Crystals

Crystals

CHANNEL THE ENERGY OF CRYSTALS FOR SPIRITUAL TRANSFORMATION

SADIE KADLEC

Contents

Foreword

Over the years, the mystery of crystals and their meanings settled into a truth known within my heart, which came into focus the moment I sat down to write the first entries in this book.

When it comes to metaphysical energy, there's nothing that can be said that we don't already know within ourselves; rather what is said is shared to stimulate reflection and build community.

Each of us has our own unique connection to the energies that surround us, and crystals are one of those many energetic forces that we gravitate towards for support, inspiration, and connection. What we may feel, or come to understand, through our relationship with crystals will always be filtered through our experiences and so only represents a slice of awareness. This doesn't make it wrong or worthless, quite the contrary - in sharing our awareness with each other, we begin to piece together a greater understanding of the whole.

Before this book was even an idea, my practice had been shifting from telling people the properties of a stone, or what stone to use, into a desire to know how a stone made them feel, what it inspired within them, and how they were going to turn that awareness into action. While you will find information about properties and uses, every word is a pouring forth of my relationship with crystals. Page by page, each entry reminded me of a person or experience in my life that perfectly highlighted that stone's energy as I've come to know it. Synchronistically, anytime I became stuck in the writing process, the crystal I was writing about held incredible guidance for that moment. Even more magically, these entries brought me into a depth of spiritual awareness that continues to influence and morph my personal practice.

My hope is that sharing these reflections with you provides a jumping-off point to deepen your own relationship with crystals. Sometimes we just need to hear someone else's experience or understanding to awaken our own. Lean on these crystal entries and practices when you are at a loss for words, or when you desire a dose of inspiration. Let them go as you find your voice.

Sadie Kadlec

Citrine page 115

Crystal foundations

Put aside everything you know about
minerals and energy. This is your time
to reflect and reconnect with your intuition
and intention before exploring the stones.
Begin anew with an awareness of a crystal's
journey from the ground to you, and the
various ways to engage and honour its
energy. Each revelation is an opportunity
to transform your relationship to the Earth,
the crystals, and yourself.

Crystal ethics

As in any field, there are challenges in ethics and
sustainability. For crystal enthusiasts, collectors,
and healers, the sourcing of stones is a major concern.

In order to grow our collections mindfully,
we must inquire – Where do these minerals
come from? Who's digging them out of the
ground? What are the methods used? And
are they harming the Earth and/or its
inhabitants in the process?

Question your sources

We must actively work towards greater
transparency and integrity when it comes
to the sourcing of stones. A great place to
start is by asking vendors to share their vetting
process for the companies they buy from, or
whether they know where and how the stones
they are selling were mined. A vendor should
be equally comfortable disclosing that
information or willing to ask the same
questions when purchasing their own supply.
Asking directly gives them the opportunity
to find out or may inspire them to be more
conscious with their next purchase.

There's no way to validate the answers we
receive and, currently, no organization exists
to monitor crystal-sourcing ethics. We really
are trusting our vendors. Having a good
relationship with them is helpful.

Investigate where you can give back

And what about all the crystals we may have
purchased already without a second thought?
It can feel disheartening to think that maybe
your new crystal has an unsavoury story. Let
that inspire you to learn more about where the
crystal is found and find ways to support those
communities and environments exploited in
the process. If you're a crystal vendor, this
would be a very powerful way to recirculate
proceeds as an act of gratitude.

While many crystals are the byproduct of
other mining endeavours, remaining aware
of how everything is ultimately connected
encourages us to reflect on other aspects of
our consumption. We may not see the land
where the minerals are mined, or the people
who dig them out of the ground. We may not
see the journey the stones take across and
around the globe to arrive at the crystal shop.
We can, however, remain aware that we are
stewards of the Earth and accept that
responsibility as a spiritual calling.

Let this inspire you to reflect more deeply
on how you build your collection and how
you can give back to and care for the Earth.

Top to bottom: Chrysanthemum Stone page 140, **Peach Moonstone** page 142, **Spessartine Garnet** page 141

Your crystal collection

A crystal collection is an ever-evolving, infinite process.
Each stone finding its way to us, intersecting with our
experiences, and leaving wisdom in its wake.

Choosing your crystals

Selecting stones can be very intimidating.
As a society, we tend to be overthinkers, and
so we question ourselves unnecessarily. Many
of us come into a crystal shop assuming we
know nothing about the crystals shimmering
on the tables. While we may have not read all
the crystal books, or studied their qualities,
we do have an energetic connection drawing
us to the stones that are meant to share
something with us. Sometimes we'll recognize
this connection by a strong reaction to the
stone, which manifests as either an instant
attraction or complete repulsion. Sometimes
it will be the description that piques our
interest. Maybe the crystal will come to us by
way of another person. However they arrive,
trust that the stones that are meant for you will
find their way to you.

Caring for your stones

Many crystal collectors often forget a crucial
component to any crystal practice - caring
for their stones! What does it mean to care
for your crystals and why should you do it? To
care for anything demonstrates appreciation,
connection, and value. We care for our stones
as a way to show respect and recognition of
the energetic exchange their vibration offers
in support of our own. Remember that the
way we care for our stones is a reflection
of how we see ourselves and represents our
respect for the energy around and within us.

Crystal cleansing

Once a mineral comes into your life, honour
its arrival with a cleansing ritual. This is not
to erase the energy that the stone may have
picked up (energy is neither good nor bad,

Left to right: **Yellow Calcite** page 139,
Bumblebee Jasper page 139

it is simply our perception of energy that changes), but to acknowledge the journey and wisdom acquired en route to us. Cleansing rituals can take many forms. Some minerals are best cleansed by other stones (Selenite or Fluorite are great options) or by being immersed in smoke (herbs, wood, or incense). Others can be cleansed through exposure to wind, being submerged in water, or buried in the earth. Use the technique that feels most in alignment with your personal practice, the mineral, and its energy.

Engaging with your stones

As soon as it is cleansed, set your intention for the stone. This could simply be by holding it and saying, "This is how I envision our work together..." or you could perform a more elaborate ritual. Choose the method that resonates the most, remembering that it is only to help clarify where you are at this moment and guide the way you will engage with the stone. Keep in mind that the crystals may have other things in store for you.

As you grow your collection, remember a key part of crystal care is regular engagement. This is the energetic action behind your intention – the way that you use them and receive their vibrational guidance and support. Meditate with them, display them, carry them with you, build grids, incorporate them into your healing sessions, wear them as jewellery. If they've been used a lot, honour all that work with a cleansing ritual, or charge them in sunlight or moonlight to add a dash of celestial energy. Engagement is all about enjoying your stones and appreciating them. Have fun!

Crystal energetics

Created in a confluence of fluid, heat, and pressure, crystals emerge with an orderly atomic structure that, quite literally, forms the foundation of our lives.

Consider the very ground beneath us, certain advancements in medicine and technology, the food that nourishes us – all rely on the existence of crystals. We too are made of minerals and need them for both our physical and energetic bodies to function. Even if you have difficulty opening up to the more mystical sides of life, crystals are there supporting you every step of the way.

Connecting to crystals
If you're ready to explore their essence further, close your eyes and breathe deeply. Sense the metaphysical energy that is all around and within you, that is you and all things. Our whole universe is flowing energy that comes together in various configurations. Some are visible, and others, like the air, we trust are there but can only feel. Crystals are tangible expressions of this metaphysical energy taking physical form and emitting a consistent, supportive vibration. While there's endless variation in a crystal's properties, all of which present differently depending on its composition, it remains true to its regular atomic pattern, forming the incredible lattice structures we admire.

Their physical and energetic constancy provides stability to us as emotional beings sensitive to the influences of the external world. When we connect to crystalline energy, we experience an energetic resonance with the crystal and recall the vibrational pitch that will bring us into harmony and remind us of our innate divinity.

Pink Mangano Calcite page 85

Bringing crystals into your life

At the deepest level, all energy is universally connected. Even though there are more than 5,000 minerals in our world, they all are descendants from the same cosmic event, which created not just our Earth but the universe, showing us how everything is a beautiful, unique expression of a single source of energy. As such, we can channel and connect to any energetic essence at any time in any place. This enables us to feel a stone's qualities without knowing the stone or having a specimen, simply by paying attention to shifts in our own energy when the stone crosses into our consciousness. Its supportive vibration is always there even if we've never seen or held that particular crystal in our hands.

Throughout this book are practices that can help you connect to crystals and find resonance in your daily life. You know best what is in alignment with your own needs and desires. These suggestions are adaptable and here to stimulate your mind to uncover your own ways and methods of embracing and channelling crystalline energy.

Crystal grids

If eyes are windows to the soul, then crystal grids are the earth's mirrors, reflecting back to us our own energy.

In the simplest terms, a crystal grid is a group of stones brought together to expand an energetic intention. While there are many methods for creating a grid, the one directed by our intuitive nature tends to be the most profound - revealing a constellation that speaks to our deepest self and offers endless guidance and support.

To create your own crystal constellation, begin with an intention, the purpose that gives context to the stones used. Take a moment to centre your energy and focus on your intention. A quick meditation with eyes closed and your crystal collection in front of you is a great way to set the space for a powerful and smooth process. Once ready, open your eyes and let your intuition select the stones and indicate where to place them. Do your best to keep the logical and rational mind from interfering, tapping into the trust and wisdom that is within you. As soon as your grid feels complete, close your eyes and take a few deep breaths before viewing the completed constellation. What sparks your attention? What do you notice about the stones, pattern, flow, and so on? Let yourself explore the qualities from a place of loving curiosity.

Create a ritual

A ritual brings your newly created grid to life. This is where your participation harmonizes the intention and crystals, together creating energetic shifts. It can be a practice as easy as meditating by the grid three days in a row, or reflecting on the energetic evolution through daily journalling. Follow your intuition to find the right practice and rhythm for your ritual.

Clockwise from top: Green Kyanite page 80, **Amazonite** page 75,
Blue Topaz page 180, **Blue Apatite** page 199, **Prehnite** page 68,
Peridot page 88, **Malachite** page 88, **Blue Fluorite** page 172,
Moldavite page 122, **Green Calcite** page 43, **Blue Calcite** (centre) page 192

The crystals

Weave through this collection of minerals
with intuition as your guide. Unearth your
very own crystalline messages buried within
each entry and deepen your connection to
the stones through the affirmations and
integrative practices. Embrace the way each
crystal shows up uniquely for you, offering
its wisdom and acting as a catalyst for your
energetic transformation.

Ammonite

"I see life with expanded awareness and embrace each moment of connection as it elevates my consciousness."

Ammonite

Elevating, Transcendent, Resilient	**QUALITY**
Root, Heart, Crown	**CHAKRA**
Energetic expansion, Transformation, Spiritual evolution	**FOCUS**

Time has a slippery way of flowing between destinations that disappear against the backdrop of life. Each moment becomes a transition from past to future, where we are held delicately in the present – simultaneously living and reflecting. It's a constant and endless process, often leaving us wondering, "Is this it? Is this all?" Where are you now in this cycle – the beginning or the end? Does life have meaning beyond this moment?

Ammonite swirls in (or is it out?) to expand perception, moving us around our experiences to gather a more dynamic awareness of the role they play in shaping our lives. We begin to see their interconnectedness throughout time and the possibilities for the future. Strengthening the ability to integrate this wisdom, Ammonite encourages our spiritual evolution by synching our energy to be grounded, present, and unfolding.

Open your eyes to those experiences you are circling around where expanded perception could help elevate you beyond them. Envision yourself as a bird in the sky, whose keen vision can assess the situation from all sides. Gracefully absorb the information to support spiritual transformation by swirling in and out and around like Ammonite.

Deepen this expansion in your daily life through moments of reflection balanced by consistent activation of spiritual energy. Include Ammonite in:
• Breathwork (see page 156)
• Mineral nap (see page 182)

EARTH

Ready to move beyond? Flip to Lapis Lazuli, page 204
For a new vantage point see Blue Tiger's Eye, page 68

Green Apophyllite

QUALITY	Renewing, Flowing, Pure
CHAKRA	Sacral, Heart, Crown
FOCUS	Remembering childhood wonder, Cultivating connection, Guiding your energetic flow

As we grow, life's routines can begin to dull our perception directing us straight into a rut. Then our energetic flow stutters. Boredom and melancholy creep in dulling the vibrancy and connection the world offers.

Transporting us to a mythical verdant land straight from our wildest and most beautiful dreams, Green Apophyllite adds a layer of sweet shimmer helping us to rediscover the world with new eyes, where everything becomes precious and magical. Curiosity heightens, our relationships brighten, and we feel a sense of renewal that breathes life into each step.

Evaluate areas where you could bring luminosity into your world. Let your eyes absorb the space around you with curiosity and playfulness. Immerse yourself in the elements to rekindle a sense of wonder for the effortless flow and mysticism embodied by nature.

Let Green Apophyllite's essence bring you back in touch with the vibrancy of life. Stimulate your sense of wonder whenever life begins to feel dim. Try using this stone in:
• Forest bathing (see page 52)
• Mineral nap (see page 182)

Go deeper with nature using Petrified Wood, page 33
Cultivate reconnection with Copper, page 191

Dendritic Agate

QUALITY	Curious, Thriving, Grounding
CHAKRA	Root, Sacral, Crown
FOCUS	Finding avenues of growth, Cultivating inner abundance, Feeling your way through

In the core of our being lie seeds of dreams we hold for ourselves slowly taking root and looking for an outlet. If the mind is given freedom to intellectualize them, they get caught in a loop, never finding their way to the surface. We begin to crave their expression but create endless blocks, inhibiting their growth and subsequently our inner abundance.

Dendritic Agate reaches within us to channel these expressions along the path of least resistance. It teaches us how to branch out from a place of curiosity so that we are constantly exploring, but not forcing our way through.

In the fern-like expression that characterizes Dendritic Agate, you'll see that not all branches lead somewhere. Let that serve as a reminder that not every seed has to become something greater; its presence alone is a direct reflection of the health of the inner environment.

Follow Dendritic Agate's lead and replace force with curiosity. Learn how to provide a nourishing environment that supports the growth of a dream, all the way through to its fullest expression. What dormant seeds lie within? Can you refrain from trying so hard to make it all happen and move back to a place of excitement?

Whenever your mind starts to take control and block a dream's growth use Dendritic Agate in:
• Breathwork (see page 156)
• Watercolour painting

For a fresh start turn to Rainbow Moonstone, page 171
Feeling curious? Find your way to Dalmantine, page 91

Green Apophyllite

"My eyes are open to
the wonder of the world.
I let the sense of awe
inspire me."

Dendritic Agate

"I nourish my dreams
and allow them to flow
through me without
resistance."

Fuchsite

QUALITY	Integrating, Nurturing, Detoxifying
CHAKRA	Heart, Third Eye
FOCUS	Opening the heart and mind, Making space for gratitude, Seeing your experiences as resourceful guides

Uncovering and discarding the roots of our pain, we tend to our inner garden by curating the parts of ourselves and our experiences that appear well put together and pleasing to the external eye. Finding great satisfaction in the culling while we attempt to create order from the chaos, we inadvertently close ourselves off to the wisdom and power that our pain offers.

Whenever we forget the immense resourcefulness that our pain inspires, Fuchsite pops up with a reminder to open the heart and mind. It detoxifies our thoughts, so we see and appreciate all of our experiences regardless of how they are labelled, and rekindles our trust in the divine.

As you tend to your energetic garden, notice the tendency to remove the reminders of painful memories. Lean into Fuchsite to bring your attention back to how those moments challenged you and inspired the ingenuity, adaptability, and creativity needed to survive. When we allow ourselves to see all experiences as integral parts of life, we create space for everything to co-exist in perfect harmony.

Integrate and embrace your experiences nightly to nurture your resourcefulness. Fuchsite supports:
- Gratitude practice (see page 78)
- Breathwork (see page 156)
- Random acts of service

Heart open? Open it more with Prehnite, page 68
Need some nurturing? Lean into Chrysoprase, page 70

Hematite

QUALITY	Supportive, Expansive, Empowering
CHAKRA	Root, Solar Plexus, Throat
FOCUS	Discovering your true foundations, Recognizing your energetic needs, Expanding your presence

A misguided notion we receive is that there is limited room for each of us to be. Our foundations can feel small and fragile, as if built upon crumbling fragments we piece together and hoard for fear they will disappear. You may shave off the excess that makes you uniquely you to fit within the confines of your tiny parcel.

Dispelling the smoke and mirrors that prevent us from taking up space, Hematite reveals the extensive support beneath, beyond what the eye can see. On discovering this endless foundation, we feel less concerned about how much space we hold in comparison to those around us, and we find the freedom to expand.

Notice where you are holding yourself back and listen to Hematite's reminder that you are supported. As your energy unfolds from its tightly wound coil, witness those hidden-away parts of yourself expand. Receive this as an invitation to be all of who you are and nothing less.

Hematite lends more expansive groundedness in:
- Walking meditation (see page 30)
- Standing barefoot on the Earth

Expand your foundation with Epidote, page 93
Discover wholeness with Kambaba Jasper, page 49

Fuchsite

"The experiences of my life are a testament to my ability to thrive."

Hematite

"There is space for me to be all of who I am."

Black Kyanite
"My shadow self is a
reminder that I am
standing in the light.
I am safe to express
my truth."

Snowflake Obsidian
"My energy is ever
flowing, I can transform
whatever feels stuck and
embrace the change
that follows."

Black Kyanite

Expressive, Encouraging, Accepting	QUALITY
Root, Heart, Throat	CHAKRA
Communicating from the depths, Bringing your shadow self to the surface, Sharing your voice	FOCUS

There are parts of who we are that we hold in shame, and experiences that we feel label us as unworthy or inferior. We navigate life eyes down with a narrative of fear around the potential that our shame may be discovered by another.

When emotions are easily triggered and spirits are low, Black Kyanite emerges from the shadows to guide us with a gentle voice through the darkness. It grounds our expression so we can fully own those experiences that cause shame. It aligns our expression to our inner truth so we may see the beauty in our shadow self.

Remember that your shadow is the result of the light shining so brightly around you revealing your magnificence. As you face your own shadow, ask yourself, "Who am I and why am I hiding?" Allow those experiences of shame to serve as a reminder of your brilliance and create a world free of the labels that "other" us.

Ground your expression whenever you feel alone and unloveable. Go deeper with Black Kyanite in:
• Breathwork (see page 156)
• Daily journalling

Fear your shadow? Flip to Black Moonstone, page 195
Let your depths be heard with Blue Jade, page 75

Snowflake Obsidian

Renewing, Clarifying, Centring	QUALITY
Root, Third Eye, Crown	CHAKRA
Cellular reset, Restoring alignment, Welcoming a new paradigm	FOCUS

Every now and again we find ourselves in a rut, keeping strictly to our routines out of comfort and fear. Lack of change, lack of flow, leads to stagnation - an energetic quicksand, inhibiting growth and dulling inspiration.

Snowflake Obsidian is formed during volcanic eruptions, a transmutation of elements through fire. Working with it allows us to undergo a personal transmutation, taking our stagnant energy and reforming it into a stronger and more empowering structure ready to embrace life. The dusting of white Cristobalite speckles restores our vibration, giving us permission to release the grip we've held on life and embrace change.

Gaze into Snowflake Obsidian and reflect on all that you see without judgment. Ask yourself what is ready to be released, what is ready to transform? Take several deep breaths with eyes closed as you release these parts of yourself. Watch your energy shift into a new paradigm.

Bring flow back to stagnant energy daily through movement and visualization exercises. Snowflake Obsidian enhances:
• Mirror gazing (see page 79)
• Massage and minerals (see page 134)

All clear? See your way to Clear Quartz, page 249
Out of sorts? Let Tiger's Eye pull you together, page 121

Green Aventurine

QUALITY Bold, Flourishing, Deepening

CHAKRA Heart, Crown

FOCUS Growing through the challenges, Cultivating courageous love, Deepening vulnerability

THE CRYSTALS

We wake up on a mission. Planning our route from A to B and then embarking on the journey. As soon as one step falls out of line with these preparations, our minds race to failure.

The challenges we experience when everything goes awry help us grow and Green Aventurine is there to ensure the growth flourishes. It reminds us that the journey is an energetic state of mind, not a path to take or a destination awaiting our arrival. Deepening our willingness to be vulnerable, Green Aventurine helps expand the possibilities of growth that our challenges provide. It keeps the energy flowing through the heart, cultivating deep and courageous love.

Every step taken out in the open off the beaten path is an opportunity for heart-centred expansion. As you move around your day, notice where you are rushing or focusing intensely on following the script. Is there room for spontaneity? Is there space to connect? Green Aventurine is here to offer a word of advice: let your heart guide you.

Green Aventurine helps expand the heart in:
- Heart flow (see page 31)
- Hand-holding meditation (see page 157)
- Breathwork (see page 156)

Green Aventurine

"I trust my heart to guide me through life. It never steers me astray."

Embrace your bold heart with Carnelian, page 116
For loving inspiration try Cobaltoan Calcite, page 72

Desert Rose
"Life's challenges
build upon my beauty.
Each experience is
a blessing."

Desert Rose

Life is filled with difficult situations and less than perfect circumstances to navigate through them. These can dredge up our insecurities, leaving us worried about what will happen after the storm. Should we press on or stop trying?

In this moment of despair, under the most conflicted of conditions with little expectation of survival, Desert Rose shows us the way – growing, petal by petal. Its ability to harness the seemingly discouraging energy of the environment teaches us how to keep going even when it is tough.

Expand your capacity to see beyond the horizon with Desert Rose at the helm. Shift your focus from worry and fear to one of learning and evolving, letting go of those outdated beliefs that hold everyone and everything back. Allow the energy of Desert Rose to remind you of your capacity to change and inspire you to embrace

Evolving, Determined, Sustaining	**QUALITY**
Solar Plexus, Heart, Crown	**CHAKRA**
Embracing change, Navigating difficult situations	**FOCUS**

the process even when it's challenging, letting each wind storm build upon your blossom.

Channel this resilient energy during the sunrise hours through quiet meditative practices. Facilitate the shift with Desert Rose in:
• Serene silence (see page 238)
• Crystal contemplation (see page 213)

Feeling determined? Move to Pyrite, page 126
Struggling with change? Flip to Peridot, page 88

Finding the foundation

Grounding is a powerful place to begin any crystal experience. We are reminded of the security and nourishment the Earth provides and can use that to support our energetic expansion. These embodiment practices offer opportunities to connect to crystalline source energy.

Stones on the body

Placing crystals on different areas of the body provides a direct, grounding connection to the earth. As each stone is unique, this practice can be done repeatedly with shifting effects. Start working with one stone at a time until familiar with the process.

- Lie down in a comfortable spot and place your chosen stone on your body.
- With each breath, become aware of where your body is making contact with the ground.
- Once you have made connection with the ground, shift your focus towards the crystal on your body, while relaxing the mind.
- Allow yourself to absorb the stone's vibration and gently note any sensations, memories, or feelings that arise.
- Stay in this mode until you feel energetically called back into the space, then express gratitude to the stone before removing it.

Walking meditation

Consciously acknowledging the minerals beneath our feet deepens our connection to the earth. The meditation is straightforward - you walk with an intention to be open to the energetic vibrations of the earth beneath you. Below are suggestions and options to expand the practice.

- Leave any electronics at home to keep your energy more attuned to the vibrations of the earth.
- Do your best to be aware of the land, elements, and creatures around you.
- Consider learning about the geology of the ground where you are walking. The experience will vary with the different types of minerals found regionally.
- You may like to walk barefoot, weather and locale permitting.
- You could walk with a destination in mind, or let yourself wander.

Heart flow

Love is an infinite vibration, the simultaneous feeling of being held, of holding, and the movement between the two. This supreme meditative practice uses the essence of a crystal to ground your heart in love.

- Sit comfortably with a straight back, eyes gently closed, shoulders relaxed, and your crystal resting in the palm of one hand, level with your heart. Begin breathing deeply.
- Take the other hand and hover it over the stone, allowing some space between it and your palm.
- Feel the vibration flowing through one palm, up the arm, down the shoulder to the heart, back into the crystal, and then flowing through the other palm to follow the same chain on the other side, creating an energetic infinity loop.
- Stay breathing like this until your body feels restored and grounded.

Sunrise or sunset meditation

The hour before dawn and dusk are seen as energetic portals. Cultivating a meditative cadence with the sun's rhythm invites its mystical energy into your life. Including crystals in this practice transforms you into the bridge between the sun and the earth, harmonizing your vibration.

- Within the hour before dawn or dusk, find a spot to sit and meditate facing the sun, with the stone you're using resting in your palms.
- Begin breathing deeply and close your eyes. Feel the sun's warm glow wash over you and notice your body being held by the earth.
- Allow each breath to expand you further both into the ground and up to the sky, envisioning yourself becoming an energetic bridge between the two.
- Notice what intuitive reflections arise, if any, before slowly opening your eyes to regard the sun and your stone with gratitude.

Sandstone

QUALITY	Layered, Infinite, Revealing
CHAKRA	All, especially Root and Sacral
FOCUS	Exploring the layers of experience, Awareness of past, Building upon what came before

THE CRYSTALS

We move through life disconnected from the wisdom layered within our bodies, catalogued through time by our ancestors and their experiences. It is an exhausting process searching for answers outside of ourselves as if there are no internal resources to guide us. We repeat the past instead of channelling the knowledge from our lineage.

Sandstone demonstrates the power in remembering, catalyzing an awareness of the past to create a foundation that will support the future. Building upon what came before, it creates clear distinctions between the past and the present, helping us to creatively shift and integrate the lessons of life. This dynamic record of trial and error enables us to learn from the layers of experience held within history and move towards action based in thoughtful awareness.

Acknowledge your past and that of your ancestors – the seen and unseen experiences, the trauma and triumphs. Explore the revelations with honesty and compassion. Are there areas you are hesitant to witness or are actively trying to avoid? There's infinite power in witnessing the past and, as Sandstone shows, as we learn from the wisdom passed down, we can make the shift to build a more conscious collective.

Integrate the wisdom of the past by becoming aware of the layers whenever you are unsure of how to proceed and are feeling triggered.

Let Sandstone inspire:
• Chakra balancing (see page 156)
• Hiking in desert regions

To explore your layers see Snakeskin Agate, page 122

Feeling infinite? Shift to Iron Quartz, page 216

Petrified Wood

Transcendent, Evolving, Mystical	QUALITY
Root, Crown	CHAKRA
Transformation over time, Rediscovering nature's mysticism, Seeing the cycle of life	FOCUS

There's a tendency to desire things to remain the same. Consistency is comforting, and when our world begins to evolve, we react with fear and see the uncertainty as a threat to survival.

Nature, however, is always moving and change is the only constant we can rely upon. Petrified Wood demonstrates the ability for the familiar to become strange, moving from a living, growing essence into that of crystallized stone. Its evolutionary process follows the transition from the physical plane into the spiritual. Petrified wood has an aura of transcendence that inspires us to live as fully as we can in the moments we have on Earth and to embrace the time when we too shall move on.

Pause for a moment and soak up your surroundings. What is changing right before your eyes? What is eager to evolve but being held back by your fear? Petrified Wood shows you the magic that occurs when you are open to transformation.

Open yourself up to energetic evolution any time you find yourself clinging to the status quo. Petrified Wood imbues extra mysticism in:
• Forest bathing (see page 52)
• Serene silence (see page 238)

Find your purpose with Honey Calcite, page 118
Rediscover nature with Green Kyanite, page 80

Orange Selenite

Warming, Sensual, Releasing	QUALITY
Sacral, Heart	CHAKRA
Unfurling the creative energy within, Deepening the senses, Finding a new day	FOCUS

Like a dream, sometimes the pieces of life do not line up perfectly or make sense. Experiences we thought had been processed or carefully compartmentalized pop up out of nowhere in a surge of emotion triggering deep wounds. Balance shaken and our minds cloudy, we respond out of pain and fear.

When we struggle to envision life outside of our deep wounds, Orange Selenite stimulates the senses to bring emotions to a place of awareness. We are anchored by its steady rhythm and feel safe in its warmth, enabling deep integration and release.

Seek out a place of stillness, allowing creative energy to find its clearest vision and reveal the ideas and inspirations that can direct you forward. Connect to the gentle hue of Orange Selenite where safety and softness, motivation and inspiration, reveal a process that nourishes you into aligned action for an energetic renaissance.

Embrace a new day and cultivate gratitude for your experiences nightly. Orange Selenite offers awareness during:
• Sunrise or sunset meditation (see page 31)
• Sense writing (see page 212)

Craving more creative flow? See Vanadinite, page 41
Embrace sensation with Red Tourmaline, page 87

See images on page 34

Petrified Wood

"Life is ever changing. When I embrace the flow I magically transform."

Orange Selenite

"My ability to find stillness enables my creativity to flow."

Sandstone

"I have the wisdom of my ancestors within me, I move forward in life blessed by their experiences."

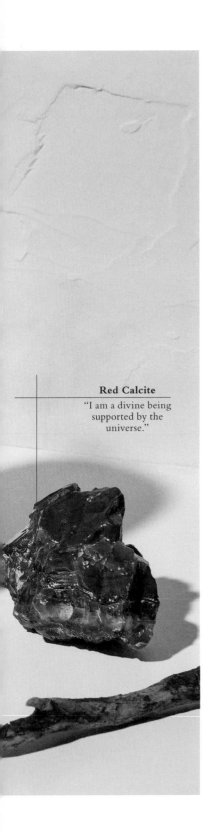

Red Calcite

"I am a divine being
supported by the
universe."

Red Calcite

Nourishing, Empowering, Monumental	**QUALITY**
Root	**CHAKRA**
Recreating the narratives of our lives, Sourcing strength from within, Feeling our divinity	**FOCUS**

How many times have we looked at ourselves and succumbed to the thought that we are small and insignificant. We so easily see the majesty in others but somehow have difficulty embracing our own divinity. Stuck in the valley looking up at the mountains it seems an insurmountable endeavour to find our way to a more expansive view.

The ground rumbles beneath us and Red Calcite emerges from the depths to empower our self-reflection. It lifts our spirits higher, giving us the wings to soar. Suddenly the monumental journey of moving from valley to mountaintop is an accessible part of our everyday experience. We see our capacity to exist at different elevations as well as in between and beyond, realizing that we are pure expressions of divine energy.

Turn the pages of your life to see where you are letting the old stories restrain your ability to fly. Expand into the limitless possibilities every moment you close your eyes as Red Calcite guides you to make the necessary adjustments to your narrative. Let the reminder of your significance enable you to soar, offering an empowering boost that deepens your connection to the divine within.

Cultivate a deeper connection to your divinity whenever you start to feel small. Red Calcite empowers:
• Divine light meditation (see page 157)
• Mirror gazing (see page 79)
• Writing about your life

EARTH

Feeling epic? Move to Barite, page 244
Remember your strength with Jacaré Quartz, page 80

Desert Jasper

QUALITY	Harmonious, Imaginative, Wholeness
CHAKRA	All, especially Root and Sacral
FOCUS	Embracing interconnectedness, Appreciating the complexity of life, Pushing beyond binary

In a world built around binaries, it can be difficult to embrace the coexistence of contradictory expressions that colour our experience. We want it to be clearly one or the other – simple and straightforward. There's no room for the complexity that defines life. We lose patience and our essence morphs into a dangerous, jagged edge.

In those moments where we are hyper-focused on our expectations of what something is or should be, Desert Jasper spins our perception, harmonizing our experience with growth and gratitude, inspiring a more encompassing way of seeing life. Complexity shifts from something we avoid to a quality that represents wholeness. It pushes beyond the binary towards a fuller expression of being and relating.

Take a step back to see the bigger picture. Witness the ways in which you try to fit your expression into the confines of a "this or that" mentality. Can you cultivate more appreciation for the dynamic qualities of life? Desert Jasper shows it is possible to hold the contradictions with love and compassion, revealing how rich and beautiful life is when you let the complexities coexist.

Rediscover a powerful sense of wholeness when the moon is full with Desert Jasper softening the tension in:
- Hand-holding meditation (see page 157)
- Chakra balancing (see page 156)
- Love notes (see page 78)

Appreciate the complexity with Thulite, page 97
To see the greater whole head to Iolite, page 192

THE CRYSTALS

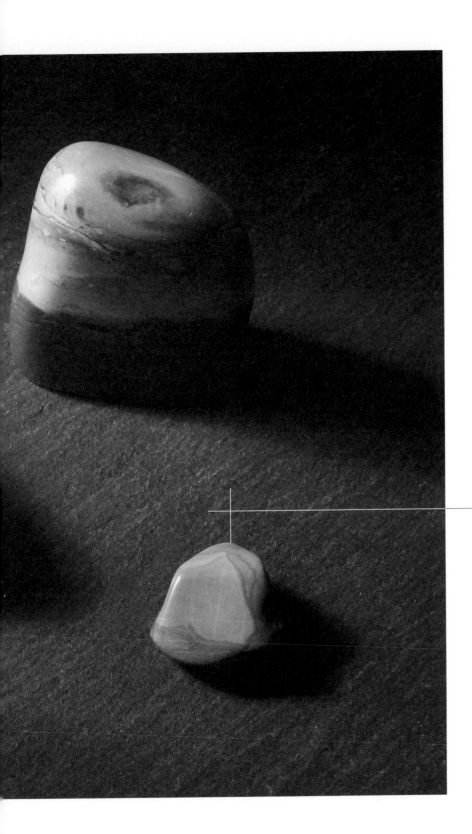

Desert Jasper

"Everything I am and feel can harmoniously coexist within the greater whole."

37

Almandine Garnet

QUALITY	Grounding, Confident, Dynamic
CHAKRA	Root
FOCUS	Finding your centre through reflection, Steady movement towards goals, Consistent energy

Plagued by uncertainty and fear, the darkest moments of our lives always feel the longest. These are moments where everything seems stacked against us, where being who we are is not enough to make it.

When we find ourselves surrounded by darkness, Almandine Garnet helps us find our centre. It whispers in our ear that the night, in all its expansive darkness, is where dreams come alive. Regardless of whether or not we have all the solutions to our problems, we can still let our dreams motivate us and inspire confidence in otherwise dim situations. Our energy, renewed by Almandine Garnet's support, empowers us to keep going even when scared or uncertain.

Identify the situations that cause you to feel off balance. How do they impede your ability to make progress towards your goals? Invite the strengthening energy of Almandine Garnet to bolster your belief in yourself and in the dreams that feel impossible during challenging moments.

Release fear and fortify your energy in times of trial. Use Almandine Garnet during:
• Crystal reading (see page 212)
• Massage and minerals (see page 134)
• Stones on the body (see page 30)

Feeling assured? Go to Moldavite, page 122
For an energy boost see Yellow Fluorite, page 119

Golden Apatite

QUALITY	Energizing, Connective, Bright
CHAKRA	Solar Plexus, Third Eye
FOCUS	Finding your fire, Inspiring your community, Letting your inner light shine

Seeing the people in our community shine and wishing for the same ability, we create a disconnect from our true self, projecting personas we believe will offer us similar acceptance and connection. It only leaves us feeling empty, alone, and unknown.

Each time we begin this cycle, comparing and searching for that which will give us the acceptance we desire, Golden Apatite lures us back with its glow to discover our own luminosity. Our awareness directed in, we finally see the strength and beauty of our inner fire. The way those around us shine becomes inspiration to let ourselves shine brightly too. Energized by this revelation, we let our radiance join others' to create beacons of inspiration that light up the whole world.

Learn to turn your gaze inward, encouraging your inner fire to burn brighter. How does it feel to glow from the inside out – to be seen as you truly are and not as a projection? Golden Apatite reveals how powerfully our collective can shine together if we each embrace our own unique glow.

Stoke your own inner flame weekly or whenever you sense an energetic flicker. Let Golden Apatite guide:
• Divine light meditation (see page 157)
• The gaze (see page 238)

Feeling divine? Float to Kunzite, page 215
Determined? Head to Rhodolite, page 101

Almandine Garnet

"I believe in myself and
my dreams. Anything
is possible."

Golden Apatite

"I am light, shining
endlessly, divine
and bright."

EARTH

39

River Rock

"Life flows around me,
I let it soften my energy
so I may move beyond
the surfaces of my
experience."

Vanadinite

"My energy is flexible,
it knows how to move
to keep itself in flow."

River Rock

Wise, Welcoming, Peaceful | QUALITY
All | CHAKRA
Acknowledging how experiences shape us, Appreciating the passage of time | FOCUS

Everything we come into contact with shapes us – the pleasant, the unpleasant, and all that falls in between. Tossed around over and over again until we are worn down, it can feel like we are victims of life's rough seas.

River Rock skips by, grazing the surface before plunging beneath, bringing our awareness with it. Polished smooth from the constant flow of water wearing away the rough edges, it glides across the planes of existence allowing us to see the way life shapes us for what is to come. We don't arrive prepared, but are blessed with the time and experiences to ensure we can handle the tides.

Notice when you have a tendency to rush. Have you given yourself time to look deeper and move with intention? River Rock represents the wisdom gained when we let life flow naturally around us. We realize that everything we experience is enabling our energy to become a softer, gentler, more compassionate vibration.

Relax into this serene energy whenever you are wanting to go deeper. River Rock lends more wisdom to:
• Water meditation (see page 182)
• Ritual bath (see page 182)

Wishing for wisdom? Turn to Wishing Stone, page 188
Stuck on the surface? Go deeper with Pearl, page 168

Vanadinite

Creative, Inspired, Spry | QUALITY
Sacral, Solar Plexus, Third Eye, Crown | CHAKRA
Strategizing, Finding your rhythm | FOCUS

Our lives are riddled with distractions. They come in a variety of forms and leave us scrambling to find the way through, back into our cadence. There's no telling when they will creep in, disrupting our flow. All we know is that, yes, it will happen.

Flow and strategy appear at first glance to be contradictory qualities, but Vanadinite combines these elements to create a highly charged vibration that empowers us to find our rhythm and let it drive our inspirations into creation. The blocks and distractions that arise become opportunities for creative expansion.

Identify where you feel more comfortable between flow and strategy. See if you can lean towards whichever one is more challenging. Vanadinite provides us with the sensibility to know how to move between the two to circumvent the typical experience that comes with distractions. Develop your own energetic dance to keep your creativity flowing and your dreams manifesting.

Inspire your imagination whenever you feel blocked. Vanadinite guides:
• Golden channel meditation (see page 238)
• Stargazing (see page 52)

Inspired? Let Soapstone guide you further, page 110
Found your rhythm? Move to Rhodocrosite, page 133

Red Jasper

QUALITY | Stabilizing, Invigorating, Nourishing
CHAKRA | Root, Sacral
FOCUS | Anchoring, Connecting with environment, Discovery

THE CRYSTALS

Have you ever had moments where it feels impossible to feel anchored while moving forwards? The struggle to break through and reach a depth that will allow you to feel supported and successful can seem elusive. Digging in the hard, red clay of the desert is like that – chipping away only to discover you've barely moved beyond the surface.

Red Jasper reminds you to pause and reassess the situation from different vantage points, absorbing all the information that surrounds you. Envision yourself rooting down, finding support and nourishment in the earth. What can you glean from your environment? Is there another approach you hadn't considered? Plants in the desert wait until the monsoon rains soften the clay soil before stretching their roots deeper. As you listen to Red Jasper's cues to appreciate the wisdom of your surroundings, you will feel invigorated to try something new, and in doing so uncover the route of least resistance to attain the stability and success you seek.

Reconnect with your environment whenever you feel restrained. Red Jasper enhances:
• Walking meditation (see page 30)
• Sense writing (see page 212)

Red Jasper
"I pay attention to the wisdom of my surroundings to uncover guidance that will support me."

Energized? Explore Abalone, page 163
Hesitant? Find encouragement with Dolomite, page 71

Green Calcite
"My energy is immense and magical, I navigate the transitions with grace and ease."

Green Calcite

Soothing, Releasing, Immense	**QUALITY**
Heart	**CHAKRA**
Softening the heart, Increasing the flow of generosity, Calming anxious spirits	**FOCUS**

We dance between instinct and emotion all day long. The transition from one to the other can cause a surge of anxiety, leading us to close off our hearts. Memories, emotions, and fears become locked within our bodies, making it difficult to exist with confidence and love.

When the mountain of life feels insurmountable and anxiety runs high, Green Calcite comes to the rescue. Its soothing aura instantly quietens our fears and imparts a sense of calm confidence. We begin to recall what it is like to simply be. Our hearts lose their stiffness and find their way back to connecting.

Stand tall as you reconnect to your immense, magical, and flowing energy. Where can you expand your essence? Where can you embody more softness? Green Calcite acts as the key to recalling the memory of our natural state of being – a place of neutrality that enables connection. It's all part of the process in reclaiming yourself. The world is waiting for you.

Find stillness and soothing as often as needed near nature. Green Calcite deepens:
• Serene silence (see page 238)
• Crystal yin yoga (see page 134)

To soften the heart see Pink Mangano Calcite, page 85
Feeling monumental? Go to Diamond, page 208

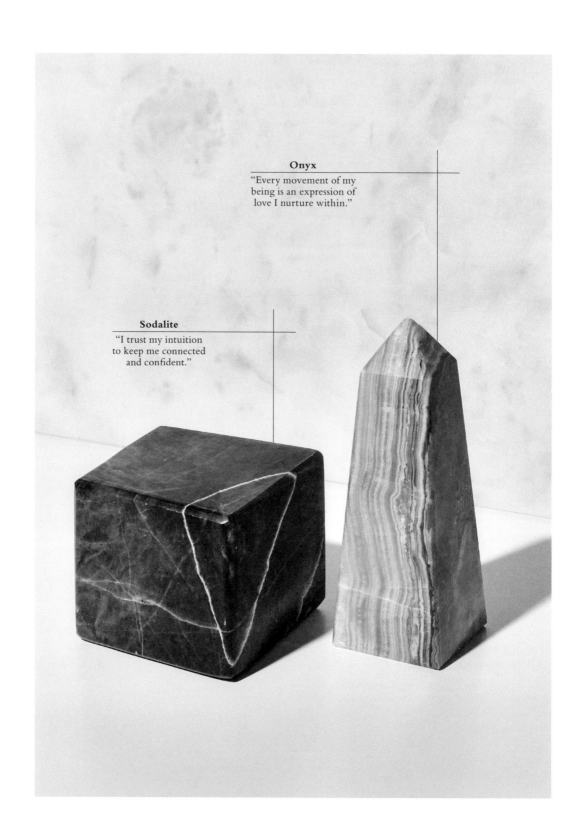

Onyx
"Every movement of my
being is an expression of
love I nurture within."

Sodalite
"I trust my intuition
to keep me connected
and confident."

Sodalite

Intuitive, Awakening, Recalibrating	QUALITY
Third Eye, Throat	CHAKRA
Developing faith, Soulful conversations, Seeing oneself as enough, Releasing worry	FOCUS

We easily dwell on the difficulties and worst-case scenarios. Our beautiful imaginations run wild creating internal dramas that the mind devours and uses to distract us from being present. How can we cultivate meaningful relationships with each other when these thoughts interfere?

Sodalite makes lightning strike within us, shocking us out of the paralysing illusions trapping us in fear. Our intuition finds its footing and guides us towards the truth where we discover that everything will be alright. We are able to breathe a little deeper and see things from a place of honest reflection.

Pay attention to when worry dominates your expression. See it as an opportunity to reconnect with your intuition and lean into truth to recalibrate your thoughts. Allow the awareness that Sodalite brings to jolt you out of the fearful fantasy. Let it usher in the belief that you are enough, that faith will pull you through.

Embody the fullest expression of intuitive guidance and connection anytime worry creeps in. Sodalite supports:
- Reiki (see page 182)
- Public speaking

Stuck in fantasy? Move to Aragonite, page 125
Ready for connection? Go to Scolecite, page 84

Onyx

Focused, Earnest, Ceremonial	QUALITY
Root, Third Eye	CHAKRA
Increasing concentration, Embodiment practices, Cultivating deeper rituals	FOCUS

We move on autopilot throughout the day, falling into habits that define us. Actions that become disconnected from their intention lose their impact and enjoyment. Making shifts out of our routine is a complicated endeavour, especially when we lack motivation or excitement.

It's not spontaneity we are craving, it's meaning in the things we do. Onyx strengthens our resolve and opens our eyes to the deeper reasons behind our actions. It helps us to make choices that reflect our intentions.

Create a clearer picture of the energy behind your actions. What is their purpose and are they supporting you? When we are able to connect with the meaning it's easier for us to find the motivation to keep going. Onyx enables us to feel this fully on a visceral level, elevating each motion of our body from one of habit and routine to that of embodied ritual. In doing so, every action becomes an expression of love and we feel nurtured.

Embody the deeper meaning behind actions whenever you fall into a mindless routine. Onyx strongly influences:
- Ritual building
- Reiki (see page 182)

Looking for meaning? See Rutilated Quartz, page 126
Need to break a habit? Head to Amethyst, page 207

Turquoise

QUALITY	Aware, Honouring, Evolving
CHAKRA	Solar Plexus, Heart, Throat, Crown
FOCUS	Reconnecting with the land, Integrating wisdom from ancestors, Appreciation

The land beneath us, both energetically and physically, makes up the foundations of our lives. We take it for granted, forgetting that it is crucial to our existence. It represents more than something to move over or live on, it connects us to our ancestors.

Turquoise reminds us to acknowledge that the past reverberates into the future. It encourages us to recognize all that has come before - geologically, ancestrally, spiritually - altering the expression and values of the current moment.

Draw lines through time connecting the elements of your essence to those in your lineage.

Are there aspects of your expression that you take for granted, not realizing they were passed down to you through endless moments of challenge, resilience, and exploration? Turquoise helps us receive the awareness from all the past periods of evolutionary experience as a gift. Deepen your appreciation of this inherited wisdom by recognizing that you too will be passing it along.

Honour this energy through regular reflections and by connecting with the land. Let Turquoise deepen your understanding in:
- Mineral nap (see page 182)
- Gardening with stones (see page 52)

Expand appreciation with Blue Fluorite, page 172
See yourself through time with Ammonite, page 21

Moss Agate

QUALITY	Uplifting, Enthusiastic, Ingenious
CHAKRA	Solar Plexus, Heart, Crown
FOCUS	Recovery, Inspiring optimism, Uncovering opportunities

Sometimes our situation can feel like an inhospitable environment. There doesn't seem to be room to expand or the right set-up to thrive. Other times we lose what offers us confidence or stability, increasing uncertainty and shifting us into a place of fear. The world can begin to feel like a cold place with no hope on the horizon.

Like the mossy tendrils thriving in stone cracks, Moss Agate offers a more enthusiastic relationship to space. We are immediately emboldened by its ingenuity and optimism, which help us see an opportunity to grow and make the most of our situation. This perspective helps us to recover when we get knocked down, finding new avenues of expansion.

Notice if you get discouraged when the spaces and situations you find yourself in seem unfavourable. Allow yourself to pinpoint what feels off. Then follow Moss Agate's lead and embrace a more enthusiastic perspective. A simple dash of optimism can reveal hidden opportunities and support that had been overlooked. Sometimes it's getting back up after falling down that brings the shift in perspective we need for inspiration.

Connect to this optimistic energy whenever you feel discouraged. Moss Agate uplifts in:
- Forest bathing (see page 52)
- Golden channel meditation (see page 238)

Feeling hopeful? Skip to Orange Calcite, page 130
Lost in the weeds? Head to Optical Calcite, page 219

Turquoise

"I appreciate the wisdom passed to me by my ancestors. Their efforts inspire my survival."

Moss Agate

"I open my eyes to the possibilities that exist all around me."

Kambaba Jasper
"I am one with
the Earth."

48

Kambaba Jasper

Grounding, Nurturing, Balancing	**QUALITY**
Root, Heart	**CHAKRA**
Connecting to the natural world, Stabilizing the spirit	**FOCUS**

We exist within a world that has disconnected itself from the elements, from nature. We feel it every moment we go outside and struggle to find stillness or silence where it should be plentiful. Our bodies crave being held by the Earth, yet its desire is drowned out by society's advances.

Seeing beyond ourselves, to the origins of life, offers us immense stability, and Kambaba Jasper brings that to us with its grounded and balancing energy. The all-seeing eyes that speckle its surface, composed of fossilized algae and bacteria from when the Earth was in infancy, impart a sense of knowing that can only come from witnessing the passing of time. We are at once cradled within the Earth and expanding out of it, completing the circle of life that binds our world.

Find the pieces of your vibration that are eager to feel held and expansive, especially those that could benefit from being seen in the context of life's rhythmic cycles. Let Kambaba Jasper rekindle your connection to the natural world. Watch as it opens your heart and nurtures your spirit so you may feel complete.

Embody this energy often while outside in nature. Kambaba Jasper grounds in:

- Stones on the body (see page 30)
- Serene silence (see page 238)
- Crystal contemplation (see page 213)

EARTH

Ready to bear witness? Turn to Hiddenite, page 72
Stoke your internal fire with Yellow Fluorite, page 119

Ruby

QUALITY	Nourishing, Empowering, Provocative
CHAKRA	Root, Sacral
FOCUS	Finding your passion, Developing inner confidence, Living with more enthusiasm

Societal expectations lead us to believe that we should play it cool, pretend that we don't care. This apathetic attitude dampens our natural joy and causes us to shy away from what interests us. How can we enjoy life and connect with others if we are always playing pretend, if we are doing things that don't light us up from within?

It takes confidence to show up as you are, to embrace life with gusto. Ruby acts as the warming embers that keep our light burning. It's a powerful force that pushes us towards our dreams and shows us how our passions are more than just things we do for fun.

Use your breath to circulate Ruby's energy throughout your body. Its forceful flow will revive you. As it nourishes every cell of your being and your confidence increases, think about how you want to show up in the world. Give yourself permission to be bold and dream big. Let your enthusiastic presence inspire others to do the same.

Channel this vital energy anytime you find yourself censoring your passion to fit in. Ruby adds extra oomph in:
- Heart flow (see page 31)
- Breathwork (see page 156)

Ruby

"My passion guides my path, my enthusiasm lights up the world."

Step it up a notch with Fluorapophyllite, page 153
Find what lights you up with Eudialyte, page 94

50

Golden Topaz

"My light shines
and when it shines
it encourages others'
lights to shine too."

Golden Topaz

Radiant, Purposeful, Enlightening	QUALITY
Root, Solar Plexus	CHAKRA
Self-nurturing, Appreciating collaboration, Connecting with your deeper intentions	FOCUS

Our inner radiance falls out of focus when our sight is directed on the shine of those around us. We keep it guarded for fear others will not be impressed by such a small glow. We forget to nourish our inner flame with acceptance, joy, and love.

Like a candle glowing, our energy burns gently within us. Golden Topaz encourages us to nurture ourselves so our inner flame doesn't fizzle out. It helps us see how even a small glow can make a big difference. It's not about illuminating the whole room with light, it's recognizing that our glow is enough to guide our way through the darkness.

Watch as Golden Topaz infuses your light with pure intentions and opens your eyes to see it with big love. Under its influence, can you notice that your glow becomes greater when you're in the presence of others? And their glow becomes greater in your presence, too? When we come together and shine purely, the light within each of us burns brighter and we can illuminate the world.

Keep your inner fire gently burning with Golden Topaz in:
• Golden channel meditation (see page 238)
• Aura meditation (see page 213)

For inner radiance see Golden Healer Quartz, page 145

To manifest your desires go to Malachite, page 88

Embracing nature

Stones enhance our connection to the nature that is us and around us, bringing the body, mind, and soul back into equilibrium with the universe. Immersing ourselves in the symbiotic mysticism of the Earth and the cosmos rekindles the natural essence inside each of us.

Stargazing

The night sky reminds us of how vast the universe is, each celestial body millions of miles away. It is only in the darkest of nights that we can see all the stars above, mirroring our own internal cosmic awakening. On a dark night, far away from city lights and preferably on a New Moon for optimum visibility, lay down under the night sky with a stone that holds personal significance placed on your body. Relax into the majesty of the cosmos for at least an hour to relish this expanded perception, where gratitude towards life and its complexity intensifies.

Forest bathing

Trees, which draw mineral nutrients up through the earth, teach us the importance of grounding before expanding. Not only is the air we breathe in their midst sweeter and cleaner, but immersing yourself in the beauty of trees is a powerful way to feel the layers of time, to remember the infinite possibilities of the world, and to nurture the soul. Simply take your favourite stones along for a walk through a forested area. Breathe deeply while moving slowly and intentionally through the trees, envisioning the mineral energy being absorbed into your being. Pause to witness each trunk, leaf, and shade of green.

Cloud watching

Similar to dreams, each cloud and the shape it takes reveals something about where our minds are in the moment. Watching clouds allows the mind to peacefully drift. Lay down in a spot with an open view of the sky and surround your body with five stones that inspire you. Enjoy the blissful and profound mind reset that occurs as you notice the shapes, memories, or inspirations that appear as the clouds roll by.

Gardening with stones

The Earth's energetic expression nourishes all living things into being. Gardening is a way to rediscover this energy. Cultivate a nuanced relationship with the minerals inherent in the soil by planting with conscious awareness, appreciating the surrounding environment, and choosing a water-safe stone to adorn the plant's base. Create your own tending ritual in line with the needs of your plants. Let it be a meditative moment wherein you see the care bestowed on the Earth synonymous with the care you take of yourself.

Clockwise from top: Turquoise page 46, **Aragonite** page 125,
Hematite page 24, **Fairy Stone** page 211, **Chiastolite** page 62,
Fire Opal page 116, **Dalmantine** page 91, **Vanadinite** page 41,
Lapis Lazuli (centre) page 204

Smoky Quartz

QUALITY	Grounding, Uplifting, Expansive
CHAKRA	Root, Crown
FOCUS	Finding your centre, Navigating transitions, Balancing chaos

There exists a tension between the spiritual and physical planes that stirs chaos into our internal vibration. Caught in transition between these forces we find ourselves at odds with the values and messaging received at both ends of the spectrum. Stuck in the middle, we are often left to wonder if it's possible to navigate between them gracefully.

Whenever we find ourselves in any sort of challenging transition, Smoky Quartz provides an anchor, keeping us tethered so the overwhelming feelings don't sweep us away. It encourages our roots to go deeper into the ground as a way to balance our expansion, ensuring our ability to thrive. With its support, we learn to embrace the duality of our experiences simultaneously, alleviating the need to bounce between the spiritual and the physical.

Smoky Quartz lifts us into a space of emotional calmness, where we can challenge duality by embodying it as a unified essence within us. Take this sense of wholeness and inner peace as the foundation you need to expand free of fear. Empowered by Smoky Quartz, explore how far your energy can reach.

Enjoy this unified energy whenever chaos attempts to disrupt your flow. Smoky Quartz harmonizes during:
- Ritual bath (see page 182)
- Mineral nap (see page 182)
- Chakra balancing (see page 156)

Feeling centred? Go to Selenite, page 223

Caught in the storm? Head to Pink Opal, page 109

Green Opal

Welcoming, Comforting, Releasing	QUALITY
Heart	CHAKRA
Cultivating hope, Healing suffering, Deepening spiritual perspective	FOCUS

Traumas we thought were so neatly packed away catch us off guard when they show up unannounced. Our first response is to turn down the lights and hide, but the old wounds are still there waiting.

When confronted with the traumas of the past, it's easy to fall into old behaviours. Green Opal clears away those negative thought patterns and emotions, creating space for a fresh perspective. It has us meet our trauma at the door laughing, inviting it in like an old friend, helping us to see how its arrival offers an opportunity for healing.

Green Opal reminds us that while our trauma is a part of who we are, the way we greet it has the potential to shift our feelings. During challenging situations, where can you welcome trauma like a friend and not a haunting memory? It may come and make a mess of your freshly healed space, but when it leaves, your perspective will deepen and you'll receive a greater sense of peace.

Cultivate this welcoming energy whenever your perspective towards healing feels tight. Green Opal guides you deeper in:
• Compassion grid (see page 106)
• Crystal yin yoga (see page 134)

Filled with hope? Go to Lepidolite, page 77
Deepen your spirituality with Azurite, page 235

Magnetite

Magnetic, Satisfying, Enthusiastic	QUALITY
Root, Solar Plexus	CHAKRA
Living life to the fullest, Nurturing our passions, Cultivating joy	FOCUS

What are the passions in your life? How do you nurture them? We are eager to feel life from that place of joy that bubbles up when we live our dreams. Yet there always seems to be an excuse lurking in the shadows - "not now", "maybe later", or "that's not accessible to me".

Every moment we spend distancing ourselves from what lights us up, we lose precious moments of joy. Magnetite reminds us that this is our one precious life to live. If we put it off until the timing's better, we may never see the day.

Make a list of all the things that light you up. How many of them have been hidden away collecting dust? Give yourself permission to take them off the shelf, to incorporate them into your life again. Magnetite teaches us how to let our passions guide us. When we let joy lead, our aura is magnetic, drawing all the serendipitous opportunities that direct the future of our lives. Our lives become an exciting adventure with a new horizon around every bend.

Embrace this alluring energy when life feels drab. Magnetite excites:
• Heart flow (see page 31)
• Creativity grid (see page 106)

Found your passion? Go to Unakite Jasper, page 232
Ready to live life? Head to Bloodstone, page 149

See images on pages 56-57

Green Opal

"It's not the absence
of pain that indicates
healing, but the way
I treat it."

Mookaite Jasper

"I move with intention
to appreciate the
beauty of life."

Magnetite

"My joy is magnetic.
It draws my desires to
me serendipitously."

Mookaite Jasper

Relaxing, Appreciative, Reflective | **QUALITY**
Root, Sacral, Heart | **CHAKRA**
Slowing down, Cultivating deeper meaning, Reorienting perspective | **FOCUS**

Smoky Quartz

"I am centred within myself, there's nothing I cannot handle."

Sometimes we move too fast. Rushing to get things done, finished up, so we can move on to what is next. In the rush we lose our foresight and our ability to connect. Everything becomes a checked box instead of a meaningful experience.

Nature never rushes. It takes its sweet time. And Mookaite Jasper, with its earthy hues and grounded vibration, shows us just how nature does it step by step. It reorients our perspective and brings us back in touch with the sweeter side of life – the one not defined by how much we do, but rather by how much we appreciate.

As you move throughout your day, take a moment to pause and reflect. Are you moving with intention and appreciation? Mookaite Jasper calms our nerves and brings us back to a neutral pace allowing us to notice the energy of our environment. If you want to lead a meaningful life, you must move slow enough to enjoy it.

Slow down your energy whenever things feel rushed. Mookaite Jasper grounds in:
• Serene silence (see page 238)
• Mineral nap (see page 182)
• Crystal yin yoga (see page 134)

EARTH

Moving slow? Turn to Hemimorphite, page 179
Find a neutral pace with Rutile, page 91

Hypersthene

QUALITY	Comforting, Quieting, Supportive
CHAKRA	Root, Third Eye
FOCUS	Hearing your inner voice, Cultivating peace, Calming the energy

The endless stimulation in the world means silence is difficult to find these days. Lacking the spaces to disconnect and hear our quiet inner knowing throws us off track. We end up searching for peace in all the wrong places.

When there's nowhere to go and we must make do, Hypersthene comforts us in its velvety energy and helps us go within. It quietens our awareness of the external world so we can journey through our inner landscape without distraction, providing us with much needed reprieve.

Listen to your inner voice. Can you hear it amidst the chatter? The supportive environments for reflection are closer than you think. Let Hypersthene calm your mind and free you from the chaos. Lean into its quiet vibration and find the peace that will enable you to hear the wisdom within.

Embrace this soothing energy whenever chaos reigns. Hypersthene softens in:
• Reiki (see page 182)
• Sense writing (see page 212)
• Stones on the body (see page 30)

THE CRYSTALS

Found your inner peace? Drift to Marble, page 187
Explore your inner landscape with Wavellite, page 172

Hypersthene

"I cultivate peace
within so my inner
wisdom can be heard."

Jadeite

"My heart is open and flowing. I see my every action as an act of love supporting energetic harmony."

Botswana Agate

"I feel peace when I step back and look at the bigger picture."

Jadeite

Wise, Tranquil, Balancing	QUALITY
Heart	CHAKRA
Developing stronger communities, Strengthening relationships	FOCUS

Occasionally, within life's constant flow, we lean heavily into excess or lack, creating imbalance in ourselves and our communities. If we stay too long in either experience the weight builds and we find ourselves stuck.

Jadeite comes to us when things are out of balance, illuminating the area that needs more attention so we may shower it with love. We receive a helping hand and remember to reach out to those who need support, building stronger relationships based on mutual respect and trust.

Allow yourself to honestly reflect on how you are showing up in your relationships. Expand the idea of relationships to include all things – animals, plants, the Earth as a whole. Is there balance in the support you give and receive from your communities? Jadeite helps us restore harmony to the energetic ecosystem with its gentle awareness. Allow its wisdom to empower you to move through life with conscious connection and thoughtful action.

Connect to this wise energy whenever life feels out of balance. Jadeite opens the heart in:
• Hand-holding meditation (see page 157)
• Gratitude practice (see page 78)

Balanced? Go to Sunstone, page 129
Develop vulnerability with Jacaré Quartz, page 80

Botswana Agate

Encouraging, Calming, Exploratory	QUALITY
Root, Solar Plexus	CHAKRA
Seeing the bigger picture, Soothing worries, Enlightenment	FOCUS

Our tendency to focus on small things, the details disconnected from the bigger picture, leaves us without a sense of scale, distorting our understanding of life. We forget there was a time when the world was one big expanse, coming into being piece by piece.

Whenever we lose sight of the context that surrounds our experiences, we tend to exaggerate their significance. Botswana Agate puts it all back into perspective, clarifying the scale and reminding us that it's the relationship to the whole that matters. When we adopt a more inclusive view we have the capacity to see things as they truly are.

Botswana Agate helps us to discover the view and we feel more open and calm in its supportive presence. With this expansive perspective, where can you add better context to your feelings and experiences? Watch your landscape become more profound as you expand out and everyday worries take up less space, fading into specks.

Cultivate a broader perspective whenever your vision gets lost in the details. Use Botswana Agate to support:
• Serene silence (see page 238)
• Mineral nap (see page 182)

To zoom out further go to Blue Tiger's Eye, page 68
Discover a new view with Amazonite, page 75

Chiastolite

"I embrace the transitions
of life with grace knowing
everything happens
in divine timing."

Chiastolite

QUALITY	Devotion, Awareness, Transitioning
CHAKRA	Root, Heart, Crown
FOCUS	Navigating grief, Recentring, Reframing loss

There are endless crossroads in life. The places where one thing ends and another begins. It takes all the courage we can muster to embrace the transition. Our fears rise as it feels impossible to make decisions when the future is unclear.

These crossroads of life push us to our emotional edge. We hold the tension in our bodies, and while time lessens the intensity, it doesn't necessarily take the pain away. Chiastolite imparts respect for what once was and helps us release the fear we hold for any uncertainty that may follow. It encourages us to take a breath and see the shift with a softer gaze.

Reframe the transitions as a meeting between the layers of your experience - a place where energy can come together. Under Chiastolite's care, the crossroads transform into a compass, with our souls as the centre. It becomes easy to navigate our way through, whether it be grief or loss or general uncertainty, when we've recentred ourselves to the guidance within.

Connect to your inner energetic compass when life feels uncertain. Chiastolite nurtures in:
- Crystal yin yoga (see page 134)
- Stargazing (see page 52)
- Divine light meditation (see page 157)

Lost in grief? Turn to Chrysoprase, page 70
Need more guidance? Go to Pegmatite, page 96

Black Tourmaline

Transmuting, Supportive, Purifying	**QUALITY**
Root	**CHAKRA**
Shifting energy, Seeing an experience from all angles, Letting go	**FOCUS**

Like malleable clay, we pick up the impressions from our interactions throughout the day. Each experience is an imprint, directly impacting how we feel and subsequently how we treat others. It can be difficult to find our way back to neutral.

When we're having trouble letting go of the influences and experiences that have pressed in deep, it's helpful to reflect on everything that's occurred. Black Tourmaline provides us with the 360-degree view, giving us the ability to wipe the slate clean. In an act of powerful purification, it presents the situation anew so we can begin fresh again tomorrow.

Pay attention to the energies you pick up throughout the day and how they affect you. Can you honour the experiences and then let them go? Black Tourmaline reminds us that much of the baggage we carry around is not ours, and by recognizing that fact alone, we can lighten our emotional load, facilitating greater empathy in our hearts.

Purify your energy every time you've been out and about. Use Black Tourmaline in:
• Walking meditation (see page 30)
• Ritual bath (see page 182)
• Chakra balancing (see page 156)

Black Tourmaline

"I let past experiences
go so I can begin again
with clear energy."

Let go a little more? Turn to Dioptase, page 105
Open the heart? Flip to Prehnite, page 68

63

Emerald
"I count my blessings and appreciate the abundance life has given me."

Cuprite
"I am truthful with my intentions."

Emerald

So often we take the blessings of our lives for granted. Our eyes are set to the greener pastures, believing them to be better than where we find ourselves. But our distance from them distorts the truth, hiding the same struggles and pains we're going through.

For those moments where we struggle or feel disappointed in life, it can be difficult to see how much we truly have. Emerald teaches us that abundance comes from within and that gratitude is the key to a happy life. It redirects our focus from what others have back to our own blessings.

There is much to be grateful for in life, and yet there are many blessings we fail to notice. Emerald helps us see all those we have taken for granted. The more we recognize them, the more they begin to overflow. The abundance fills our hearts and minds, instilling in us a sense of contentedness.

Balancing, Grateful, Content	QUALITY
Heart	CHAKRA
Counting our blessings, Finding true abundance, Seeing life from a magical perspective	FOCUS

End each day with gratitude and watch it reveal how truly beautiful and magical your life is.

Cultivate a grateful heart every morning and every night. Emerald deepens:
- Gratitude practice (see page 78)
- Chakra balancing (see page 156)

Struggling with jealousy? Go to Fairy Stone, page 211

Feeling grateful? Turn to Girasol, page 165

Cuprite

It's easy to make a promise. We do it all the time. The challenge is keeping the promises we make. There's fear in being held accountable for our actions. That fear stems from the obligation to be productive and prove our worth. We over-promise because we think it's what others expect. Instead, it only causes us to become overwhelmed.

In trying to please others, we disconnect from our truth. Cuprite brings us back to a place of honest communication so we can engage and act with thoughtfulness. We say things we mean and only commit to what we can truly deliver, and in the process we build deeper trust.

Take a closer look at the promises you make to others. Can you let Cuprite's thoughtful energy empower you to be more honest with what you're capable of? Receive its awareness as an invitation to embrace more accountability into your life.

Reflective, Realistic, Vulnerable	QUALITY
Root, Sacral, Heart	CHAKRA
Accountability, Thoughtful action, Honest communication	FOCUS

Watch how being open and vulnerable in this way strengthens your relationships and reduces your stress. Cuprite supports vulnerability in:
- Love notes (see page 78)
- Hand-holding meditation (see page 157)
- Heart flow (see page 31)

Time to own your actions? See Shattuckite, page 112

Connect compassionately with Blue Kyanite, page 185

Staurolite

QUALITY	Aligned, Purposeful, Patient
CHAKRA	Root, Crown
FOCUS	Connect the inner and outer worlds, Ground your energy, Discover your life's intention

The world with its endless movement and evolution can feel like a very unsettled place. We naturally crave security and stability, searching for the people, places, and experiences that evoke those feelings. There's a whisper from our inner knowing to ground down.

When the movement of the outside world feels too much, we can always go within. Staurolite marks the point where our inner world and outer world meet energetically. This allows us to find our centre and reconnect to the seed of intention that gives our life greater meaning. It reminds us of our purpose, our anchor, our why, the thing that keeps us grounded when everything else feels lost in chaos.

Let yourself discover what it feels like to be truly secure within yourself. Close your eyes and quiet your mind so that your intention has room to be seen. Staurolite gives us the patience to pay attention to the whisper within and the resolve to respond with aligned action. As you listen to this part of yourself speak, can you make the promise to live your purpose with integrity?

Cultivate true alignment and groundedness daily. Staurolite settles the aura in:
• Mirror gazing (see page 79)
• Chakra balancing (see page 156)
• Daily meditation

Find your purpose with Spirit Quartz, page 225
Go beyond the ground with Crazy Lace Agate, page 102

Brookite

QUALITY	Flowing, Reconnecting, Embodied
CHAKRA	Root, Crown
FOCUS	Bridging energetic gaps, Energizing the spirit, Awareness of the present moment

The tangible parts of our reality dominate our minds. We focus so much on what we can see, hear, and touch that we forget about what we can feel energetically. A separation between the physical and the spiritual realms manifests and leaves us feeling incomplete.

The more we rely on the physical frame of reference, the more difficult it becomes to tap into the intangible and mystical essences of our energy. Brookite's invigorating vibration brings us into a state of pure presence, having us pause so we can experience the unique feeling of each energy centre and receive its healing.

Explore the flow of your vibration. Follow it through your body as it swirls into, out of, and around each energy centre. Take note of where the flow stutters or gets caught up. These are the areas where Brookite can help you go deeper and reconnect. Embrace Brookite's flowing energy to bring you back in touch with the intangible essences of life. It's when these are connected to the tangible we remember our wholeness.

Whenever something feels stalled and needs a gentle push, use Brookite to facilitate:
• Chakra balancing (see page 156)
• Sense writing (see page 212)

Feeling present? Go to Danburite, page 205
Missing something? Turn to Stibnite, page 150

Staurolite

"I live my purpose
with integrity."

Brookite

"My energy is ever
flowing. I am with it
wherever it goes."

Prehnite

QUALITY	Connective, Opening, Supportive
CHAKRA	Heart, Third Eye, Crown
FOCUS	Redistributing energy for balance, Expanding the heart, Soothing the mind, Protecting your energy

There is an innate competition between the rationale of the mind and the desire of the heart, each vying to lead the direction our lives take. The tension causes us to doubt ourselves and make decisions under pressure and out of fear.

Prehnite steps in to mediate, highlighting the spot between the heart and mind where wisdom can be gained through collaboration. Its message is clear: synergy is not about one or the other taking charge, but in heart and mind coming together to strengthen the whole.

In those moments where you feel the pull between the heart and the mind and are struggling to decide, pause to find the neutral ground. Prehnite, with its supportive connectivity, will create the space within to encourage energetic collaboration. The notion of right or wrong disappears when the strengths of both energies are welcomed and given space to shine. Progress is exponential and aligned when heart and mind are working together.

Find your energetic equilibrium with Prehnite's opening vibration in:
• Breathwork (see page 156)
• Heart flow (see page 31)

Stuck in the mind? Go to Lapis Lazuli, page 204
Expand your heart with Rose Quartz, page 176

Blue Tiger's Eye

QUALITY	Liberating, Discerning, Empowering
CHAKRA	Heart, Throat, Solar Plexus
FOCUS	Finding motivation to act, Developing self-confidence, Expressing truth, Discernment

Our hearts desire acceptance, the feeling of being known and loved. As we project our expression onto the world around us, sharing what we assume will grant our heart's desire, our thoughts, feelings, and words become distorted from our truth. The space between who we are and who the world sees deepens.

As the disconnect grows our expression becomes paralysed and we become stuck using the expectations of others to guide what we do, share, and say. Blue Tiger's Eye highlights where we have relinquished our truth in favour of appeasing. It guides us from the out-of-body vantage point back within, helping us find our way back to authentic expression.

Acknowledge the disconnect in who you are and who the world sees. How great is the space between the two and how does that leave you feeling? Blue Tiger's Eye offers a reclamation of truth, empowering you to communicate what you really feel and to share from a place of inner strength. Every moment we choose to let our truth shine, we are able to be seen and loved for who we are, allowing us all to break free from the lies that bind.

Prompt serene knowing with Blue Tiger's Eye whenever you need to reveal truth, through:
• Mineral nap (see page 182)
• Wishing ritual (see page 79)

Embrace your glow with Aragonite, page 125
Struggling to share? Open up to Blue Kyanite, page 185

Prehnite

"Guided by my breath, heart and mind come together supporting me in all I do."

Blue Tiger's Eye

"My truth inspires the truth of those around me. Their truths inspire mine."

Chrysoprase

QUALITY	Comforting, Reinvigorating, Nourishing
CHAKRA	Heart, Root, Crown
FOCUS	Navigating intense emotions, Finding comfort after challenging experiences, Personal growth

Life is a complicated experience. One moment things are up and the next they are down. The more intense and unruly emotions (grief, loss, anger, fear) we feel, the more afraid we become of what's ahead, urging us to numb out instead of emotionally processing.

Numbness doesn't stop life from moving on, rather it takes us away from experiencing a life worth living. Chrysoprase reintroduces us to the cycles of life, helping us find comfort and meaning even in the most challenging of times.

Intense feelings will come in life – can you appreciate the moment and let it transform you? Whenever the challenges feel overwhelming, call upon Chrysoprase – its comforting vibration will help you lean into your emotions, releasing the fear that keeps you locked and detached. Under its gentle wing, we rediscover the mystical flow life takes and our souls receive the nourishment needed to make it through the trying times.

Create a supportive energetic environment with Chrysoprase in:
- Hand-holding meditation (see page 157)
- Stones on the body (see page 30)

Chrysoprase

"I choose to feel deeply. My feelings are reminders that life is significant, complicated, and beautiful."

Navigate tough times with White Agate, page 189
Growing pains? Find soothing with Tanzanite, page 191

Dolomite

"I am always learning and growing, it is OK to not know it all right now."

Dolomite

Confident, Aware, Relaxed	QUALITY
Third Eye, Sacral	CHAKRA
Reducing stress, Feeling comfortable with the unknown, Cultivating emotional honesty	FOCUS

We've all felt the rush when an answer is expected of us and the one we have isn't good enough. Maybe we don't have an answer at all. We keep talking in circles to distract from our discomfort of not being able to respond with confidence.

There's a certain pressure to produce, explain, clarify, or justify. Each one makes our stress levels rise. Dolomite releases the steam from our system, slowing us down and shifting us from a defensive position to one of emotional honesty. In the process, we learn to take the time we need to think more deeply. We learn it is OK to not have all the answers.

When we feel pressured it's easy for us to respond out of alignment. As you encounter situations where you don't know the answer, take a cue from Dolomite's relaxing vibration and pause.

Let your body, mind, and spirit harmonize so that your expression is one of integrity. Be courageous enough to say "I don't know" and watch your stress lessen and confidence grow.

Release pressure with Dolomite during:
• Crystal yin yoga (see page 134)
• Serene silence (see page 238)

Afraid to be wrong? Head to Sphalerite, page 150
Enhance confidence with Clear Apophyllite, page 207

Cobaltoan Calcite

QUALITY	Activating, Initiating, Transforming
CHAKRA	Heart, Solar Plexus
FOCUS	Deepening friendship, Opening up to love, Moving on from rejection

Humans are social creatures whose lives are built around relationships with others. That hunger for connection, to find and experience love in all its forms, can come to a screeching halt when our underlying traumas and fears pop up, dampening the flames.

The loving spark has to land on some kindling for the fire to burn. Cobaltoan Calcite shows us how to create an environment for love to thrive by making us aware of the habits, behaviours, and traumas that interfere with this. A fresh perspective facilitates the actions necessary to open up to love.

When you desire love and connection, but don't seem to be receiving it, inquire within as to where you may be closing off your heart. Cobaltoan Calcite activates healing on a deep soul level to soften the rough edges of your energy and bring in more loving awareness. We are able to see where and how to be more present in our relationships and move on from those that have run their course. Love begins to flow like a river and we are open enough to enjoy the ride.

Bring a quick jolt of loving awareness by using Cobaltoan Calcite in:
• Heart flow (see page 31)
• Hand-holding meditation (see page 157)
• Reiki (see page 182)

More love please! Turn to Pink Tourmaline, page 94

Heart stuck? Move to Scolecite, page 84

Hiddenite

QUALITY	Revealing, Content, Renewing
CHAKRA	Heart, Solar Plexus
FOCUS	Finding yourself, Rediscovering your heart, Feeling complete

There are those moments when everything feels "off" without explanation. We feel this emptiness inside us and become desperate to fill it, searching for the one thing that will provide the sensation of wholeness, not knowing exactly what it is or where to find it.

We go about life searching high and low, eyes scanning for any discernible glimmer. Little do we know what we're looking for has always been within us. Hiddenite guides our eyes directly to it. The place where we discover the expansive fullness that nourishes us in the way we need.

All it takes is awareness of our very own heart! If you find yourself searching for that sense of wholeness, ask yourself why you haven't thought to look within? Have you forgotten to look at your own heart? Hiddenite's gentle nudge in the right direction helps us recover whatever we are missing. It brings us back into heart-centred harmony so we may feel full and at ease.

Use Hiddenite to keep the heart expanding and the spirit feeling full in:
• Sense writing (see page 212)
• Mineral nap (see page 182)

Open heart? Expand further with Fuchsite, page 24

Remember your worth with Golden Apatite, page 38

Cobaltoan Calcite
"I take a deep breath
and open my heart to
love in all its forms."

Hiddenite
"My energy is centred
around my heart,
I am full."

73

Watermelon Tourmaline

QUALITY	Joyful, Releasing, Uplifting
CHAKRA	Heart
FOCUS	Heart-centred activation, Rediscovering joy, Inspiring energetic effervescence

During challenging times, it can be increasingly difficult to feel joyful. Our sight hones in on the turbulence and intensity and we lose the ability to recognize the joy in our lives. We feel heavy and depressed, the heart disconnects from the spirit, and our lives lack passion and meaning.

Joy is an energetic state of being, the alchemical reaction of gratitude and authenticity that we experience when in alignment with ourselves. Watermelon Tourmaline acts as a catalyst for rediscovering joy by bringing in the sweet, heart-centred resonance that stimulates our vibration into harmony with all aspects of our body, mind, and soul. Its presence is an effervescent boost to our energy.

Notice what inspires every flutter of joy within you. Are there specific people, places, or experiences that increase this sensation? Connect with Watermelon Tourmaline to help tickle your senses and remind you of where and how you feel joy. As you identify the circumstances that uplift you, remember to express your appreciation.

Use Watermelon Tourmaline to cultivate energetic effervescence during:
• Laughter
• Breathwork (see page 156)

Take joy to the next level with Ruby, page 50
Find your heart centre with Pink Halite, page 185

Amazonite

There's a common thread that runs through each of us - the desire to be seen, loved, supported, and to have our lived experiences recognized. We often desire this just for ourselves, forgetting that these are basic energetic rights everyone is entitled to and deserves. Our energy, hyper-focused on ourselves, becomes inflexible and conditional, creating otherness and stereotypes.

Amazonite expands our sight so we see life through the collective, not just through our own eyes. We are able to acknowledge where internal biases have blinded us and caused others harm. We find the confidence and strength to stand up for ourselves and share our lived experiences. The compassionate energy Amazonite emits brings us back to a place of humanity, where we remember our common ground and come together out of love.

Opening, Compassionate, Endless	**QUALITY**
Heart, Throat, Third Eye	**CHAKRA**
Healing through unconditional love, Community support, Acknowledging interconnectedness	**FOCUS**

If we love first and share from our heart we increase the possibility for outdated paradigms to shift. Amazonite helps us open our hearts and minds so we may welcome world peace.

Use it to facilitate a gentle heart opening in:
• Divine light meditation (see page 157)
• Reiki (see page 182)

Deepen your love with Rhodocrosite, page 133
Shift the paradigm with Grape Agate, page 227

Blue Jade

Our expression is a powerful force. If we have not embraced its power, we can feel overwhelmed by its impact. We may begin holding ourselves back, thinking it is better for everyone if we keep this energy inside, only to feel the pressure build from the containment.

When we hold back, we create imbalance in the natural flow of life. Blue Jade's rhythmic energy shows us how to honour our expression, allowing it to be welcomed regardless of its intensity. We come to respect the way the world is shaped by the collective sharing of truth and see the importance in expressive vulnerability.

Follow the ebb and flow of your expression. Where do you contain yourself out of fear that you may overwhelm the world around you? Blue Jade empowers us to embrace the reality that our truth is significant and is meant to impact the world.

Rhythmic, Powerful, Expressive	**QUALITY**
Throat, Heart, Solar Plexus	**CHAKRA**
Asserting yourself, Cultivating acceptance, Finding your rhythm	**FOCUS**

Our truth is our wisdom, and our wisdom is a gift to be given.

Embrace Blue Jade's energy in:
• Water meditation (see page 182)
• Ritual bath (see page 182)
• Singing

Find your truth with Blue Kyanite, page 185
Embrace your power with Yellow Fluorite, page 119

See images on pages 76-77

Lepidolite

"My heart opens,
I receive guidance
from the universe and
remember my divinity."

Blue Jade

"The rhythm of
my soul guides my
expression."

Lepidolite

Soothing, Enlightening, Attuned | **QUALITY**
Heart, Crown | **CHAKRA**
Energetic education, Connecting to the universe, Remembering our divinity | **FOCUS**

Watermelon Tourmaline

"Joy resonates from every cell of my being."

Amazonite

"I offer the world my unconditional love."

When we are born we know everything about the universe; we speak the language of the stars, our purpose and path are clear. Slowly we assimilate into the reality of the world, our innocence replaced with ABCs, our expression distorted to fit into society. We can forget our purpose, waking up thinking "I know I'm here for a reason, but I can't remember why."

The heart hurts losing the connection to its divinity. Lepidolite assists our journey home, easing the ache in our hearts and offering serenity. It shares the secrets that guide our way to the energetic library where we reconnect with the ancient wisdom of time and space.

Where are you in the process of remembering? When you wake up from the dream grasping at the lines, shapes, and colours from the beyond, Lepidolite's lessons in heart-held wisdom keep you attuned to the intuitive whispers of the divine. We may never fully remember the language of the cosmos, but we know enough to get by, we know enough to find our home.

Use Lepidolite to connect to the divine in:
• Mineral nap (see page 182)
• Forest bathing (see page 52)
• Stargazing (see page 52)

A I R

Uncover your purpose with Optical Calcite, page 219
Connect to the cosmos with Iron Quartz, page 216

Transcendent heart

Love, gratitude, and hope expand our capacity to connect with compassion, but are often more easily expressed to others than to ourselves, stuttering the flow of love within the heart. Each practice below is an opportunity to explore where we get stuck and to move through it with grace.

Gratitude practice

Cultivating moments of gratitude provides a clear perspective that keeps us buoyant during turbulent times. A daily gratitude practice transforms our life, revealing silver linings, inspirations, and opportunities we wouldn't have otherwise seen.

- Choose a stone that represents optimism or gratitude for you.
- Lying down with eyes closed, place the stone on your third eye, the point on your forehead between the brows.
- Maintain a natural and relaxed breathing pattern as you begin to think about all that you are grateful for.
- Keep reflecting for five minutes if possible.
- Notice what emerged when you allowed your gratitude to expand. Express gratitude to the stone before removing it.

Love notes

This practice helps us nurture our own well of self-love. Write yourself love notes anytime your heart feels hungry for appreciation, or for those times where you need a reminder of why you are wonderful.

- Choose your stone and take a few moments to centre your spirit with meditation.
- Once you feel calm and centred, take a piece of paper and begin writing yourself a letter filled with loving words. Let your expressions of love be expansive, fun, and imaginative. Reflections on your qualities you most appreciate is a great place to start.
- When you have finished writing it, sign it with a "love, me" and read it aloud.
- How does what you wrote make you feel? Where do you feel it in your body? Let this inspire you to nurture yourself with love.

Mirror gazing

Mirror gazing encourages us to let our reflection highlight where we can hold ourselves with more love. This practice can be uncomfortable at first, but keep with it to see and feel the transformative effects.

- Find a mirror you can use to sit and stare at your reflection.
- Sit down in a comfortable seat, close your eyes, and, with your stone in hand, take a few deep breaths before opening your eyes to your reflection.
- Look at yourself with love, as much love as you can muster. Do your best to refrain from criticizing your image.
- Start with small increments of time and work your way up to longer periods, noticing subtle changes in your comfort or ability to keep your judgments at bay.

Wishing ritual

To make a wish is to bring a hidden desire up through your heart and surrender it to the universe for manifestation. This practice illuminates your deepest desires and gives them space to become a part of your reality.

- Find a comfortable place to lie down, with your chosen stone either on your body or held in your hands.
- Breathe deeply and give yourself permission to hope and dream. Welcome whatever surfaces and keep breathing it from within you into your stone.
- Once you've identified your wish and connected it to your stone, hug your stone to your heart with love and gratitude.
- Every day find a moment to hug your designated stone and reflect on your wish. Listen as the crystal whispers its wisdom.

Jacaré Quartz

QUALITY	Multi-dimensional, Revealing, Vulnerable
CHAKRA	Crown, Root, Heart
FOCUS	Revealing what is hidden, Appreciating complexity, Letting the soul shine

Our soul wants to be seen and to share its unique beauty. Yet, society favours us when our expression is easy to digest in a quick, shallow view. We hide the multi-dimensionality of our soul so that we can be easily understood and widely accepted.

Every moment we repress our vibration we lose touch with our magical complexity, the essence that makes us shine. Jacaré Quartz's empowering energy reminds us of our beauty and worth. It helps us find our way through the inner labyrinth we created to keep ourselves contained and safe from the critical eye of the world.

What is hidden within you? Are there pieces of who you are waiting to be shared? Hiding any part of ourselves keeps us from being known, hindering meaningful connection. Jacaré Quartz lifts our spirits through an energetic reckoning, inviting what has been suppressed to the surface. We rediscover our magical essence as the story of our soul is told.

Bring to the surface what's hidden with Jacaré Quartz in:
• Mirror gazing (see page 79)
• Gratitude practice (see page 78)

Find your magic with Amethyst Flower, page 215
Shine your soul with Rainbow Fluorite, page 231

Green Kyanite

QUALITY	Opening, Cleansing, Calming
CHAKRA	Heart, Throat
FOCUS	Finding your truth, Soothing anxiety, Connecting with nature

There's an art form in listening from the heart. It is what allows us to pick up and appreciate each unique sound. The receptivity we practise while listening teaches us how to be in tune with the needs of our communities.

Nature is the ultimate symphonic training ground. Even in the silence there is a sonic vibration. If we open our hearts, we can hear even the faintest energetic whisper. Green Kyanite helps us hone our ability to truly listen, to pick up the truth that is struggling to be heard amongst the noise.

Listen to the sounds of your own heart. Can you hear its gentle beat? Are you aware of what it is sharing? Commune with nature and practise the art of listening. Go deeper with Green Kyanite to hear the sounds beneath the sounds, to witness the rustling of energy. When we are open and receptive to the subtlety, we rediscover the hidden beauty.

Use Green Kyanite to embrace nature's calm energy in:
• Forest bathing (see page 52)
• Gardening with stones (see page 52)
• Massage and minerals (see page 134)

Hear nature's wisdom with Green Apophyllite, page 22
Move stagnant energy with Blue Tourmaline, page 184

Jacaré Quartz

"I welcome to the surface all the hidden magic within, I let my soul shine."

Green Kyanite

"In nature I see my truth alive and well."

Ajoite

"I cultivate stillness within so that I may hear the whispers of my soul."

Strawberry Quartz

"My appreciation illuminates the miracles of life."

Ajoite

An underappreciated beauty is the stillness found in moments alone. These are the experiences where we are able to cultivate a quiet breath and raise our spiritual vibration. We receive the spiritual attunement that only arrives when we cultivate a sincere relationship with our inner spirit.

The world is growing louder, the distractions are increasing and it's difficult to find space to be alone in our own energy. Ajoite creates a protective orb that drowns out the external chatter to connect us to our higher self. It cultivates stillness so we can hear our intuition whisper to us.

Transcend the static of your life by embracing the quiet moments as they come. What secret messages do you hear when you let the outside noise fade away? The stillness that we find with

Refreshing, Intuitive, Calm	QUALITY
Crown, Third Eye, Heart	CHAKRA
Self-discovery, Spiritual evolution, Appreciating the quiet moments	FOCUS

Ajoite encourages radical self-discovery. When we know ourselves more intimately, we become ready to evolve spiritually.

Cultivate self-discovery with Ajoite in:
- Serene silence (see page 238)
- Mineral nap (see page 182)

Busy mind? Meander over to Howlite, page 220

Intuition fuzzy? Flip to Blue Chalcedony, page 163

Strawberry Quartz

Our perception of life is that it needs to be immense and grand for it to be meaningful. Without the epic there is no transformation. We expect the pomp and if it doesn't arrive, our spirit dims with the disappointment.

Whenever we forget to appreciate the small things and see their relationship to the greater whole, Strawberry Quartz waltzes in to bring everything back into focus. We witness the way the small moments connect to create the larger narrative of life. Suddenly the ordinary becomes extraordinary.

Open your eyes to the everyday miracles that make life the epic experience that it is. Does that create space for you to enjoy life more? Strawberry Quartz helps us find pleasure in the simple things by teaching us the art form of gratitude. Appreciation transforms the mind,

Considerate, Simple, Meaningful	QUALITY
Third Eye, Heart	CHAKRA
Creating rituals out of the everyday, Appreciating the magic of life	FOCUS

bringing life into focus so our eyes can see the magic that is all around us.

Open your eyes as regularly as possible with Strawberry Quartz during:
- Gratitude practice (see page 78)
- Walking meditation (see page 30)

Appreciative? Turn to Fluorapophyllite, page 153

Feeling jaded? Head to Jadeite, page 61

Scolecite

"I allow love to flow spontaneously from the deep well of my generous and compassionate heart."

Scolecite

QUALITY	Generous, Spontaneous, Connective
CHAKRA	Sacral, Heart, Throat
FOCUS	Fostering connection, Expressing appreciation, Cultivating a free flow of love

There are times when the sting of rejection or hurt encourages us to close our hearts. Fear finds its way into our bodies, restricting the breath and feeding the feelings of disconnection. But how does your body feel when compassion is flowing freely through your aura?

Scolecite, like gentle rays of sunshine filtering through on a cloudy day, inspires spontaneous bursts of love to emanate from the core of our being towards the world around us. It teaches us how to offer what we seek, to be that which appears lacking. In doing so, we become a co-creative force, adding infinite beauty and connection into the world. If Scolecite took physical shape, it would be an infinity symbol.

Whenever fear rises and your energy closes off, receive the experience as an invitation to spontaneously shower yourself with love. Do the same for others and watch the contagious effect of kindness create harmonious ripples.

Integrate Scolecite into your life through regular practice, on days when the sun is streaming through the clouds, with:
• Love notes (see page 78)
• Random acts of kindness
• Hand-holding meditation (see page 157)

Opened? Expand with Snakeskin Agate, page 122
Fearful? Tap into Carnelian, page 116

Pink Mangano Calcite

Softening, Integrating, Empathetic	QUALITY
Solar Plexus, Heart, Crown	CHAKRA
Soothing self-criticism, Seeing yourself as an integral part of the greater whole	FOCUS

As energetic beings existing in the physical reality of time and space, it is inevitable that we experience moments of guilt, shame, and unworthiness. Our critical eye turns inward and hones in on the aspects that seem unacceptable. We bury them deeply for fear of rejection.

When we feel lost in a stormy sea, Pink Mangano Calcite envelops us in the gentle pink waves of its energy, soothing our aching souls. Tension softens and we are emboldened to let go of the limiting beliefs we've held onto for so long. We begin to see how all the facets of our being make us who we are, and provide us with information on which direction to grow.

Explore where you can invite more softness or acceptance into your life. Can this be directed equally in all directions – towards yourself and outwards to those around you? Pink Mangano Calcite invites us to see how our deepest shame is also the source of our greatest empathy. Allow the energy of this stone to support you in integrating all parts of yourself – without judgment – and cultivating profound empathy in all of your relationships.

Use Pink Mangano Calcite to soften in:
• Ritual bath (see page 182)
• Breathwork (see page 156)

AIR

Pink Mangano Calcite

"I see all parts of myself
as significant and
deserving of love."

Eager for more peace? Flow to Selenite, page 223
Can't let go of the pain? Move to Chrysoprase, page 70

Red Tourmaline

"As I allow the layers of
my trauma to unwind,
peace follows."

Petalite

"Flower buds open in
their own time and
so do I."

Petalite

Flower buds do not arrive fully bloomed and neither do we. Each experience is a gentle unfolding. A response to conditions of our environment and our readiness to open. It takes energy, time, and opportunity to transform. If we try to rush the process, to move faster than we are ready or faster than our environment will allow, we exhaust our energy.

Patience may be challenging to muster, especially when it feels like the rest of the world is moving so much faster and further than us. Petalite helps us adhere to divine timing, guiding us so we arrive precisely at the moment where everything aligns. It cultivates patience, and helps transform the nature of our daily habits from routine into ritual. We learn to appreciate the experience and what it reveals within us as much as the destination.

Softening, Accepting, Ripe	QUALITY
Heart, Solar Plexus	CHAKRA
Slowing down, Cultivating patience, Enjoying the process	FOCUS

Petalite opens our awareness and inspires a willingness to accept where we are in the moment without frustration.

Let the divine guide your blossoming in:
- Love notes (see page 78)
- Crystal yin yoga (see page 134)

Ready to bloom? Open to Spessartine Garnet, page 141

Transform routines with Rutilated Quartz, page 126

Red Tourmaline

Our physical bodies hold every memory, from those passed down through our lineage to the baggage from our lived experiences. Having held such contorted forms for so long, we have begun to believe this is what life is supposed to feel like, deepening the twist that restricts our freedom.

Healing feels uncomfortable as we become aware of parts that have long been numb. Red Tourmaline unwinds us on all levels, pushing our pressure points and awakening us to a way of life that feels better. It brings sensation back into our bodies and with it the awareness of our attempts to protect ourselves from harm.

Reflect on the way you have contorted your body to make it through difficult experiences. Where is more healing needed to transform the traumas that cause heaviness on the heart? Even

Somatic, Sensory, Persistent	QUALITY
Root, Sacral, Heart	CHAKRA
Recovering from trauma, Restoring sensation, Healing inter-generationally	FOCUS

when we don't see results immediately, Red Tourmaline's vibration inspires us to keep going. It reminds us we spent a lot of time twisting and it's going to be another journey to unwind.

Resolve deep trauma with Red Tourmaline in:
- Massage and minerals (see page 134)
- Crystal yin yoga (see page 134)

Unwind your perspective with Gwindel Quartz, page 220

Come back into your body with Staurolite, page 66

Malachite

QUALITY	Inspiring, Fortuitous, Trust
CHAKRA	Heart, Solar Plexus, Throat
FOCUS	Co-creating with the universe, Listening to the divine, Flowing with life

Our expectation is that A must lead to B and we prepare for what is in between. We mould our visions according to the realities we see, around the way that life has already flowed. All that focus is an attempt to override the majesty and magic of the universe.

We forget that life operates under a different set of rules where there are infinite possibilities and permutations. Our imagination is often limited by what we believe to be true, and we miss the opportunity for expansion offered by all that is out of sight. Malachite has a way of getting us to stray from the standard path. Its energy is a whispered invitation of curiosity encouraging us to take the road less travelled.

Listen to the divine directions. Can you trust the universe even when you can't see what's around the bend? Every green swirl of this stone is a reminder of life's organic flow, and when we are willing it will take us on a spiritual adventure. Malachite encourages us to communicate the desires held within the heart, even when they seem impossible, because the universe is always listening.

Shift energy with Malachite in:
• Wishing ritual (see page 79)
• Walking meditation (see page 30)
• Divine light meditation (see page 157)

Listen to the divine. Choose a random page
Trust issues? Turn to Danburite, page 205

Peridot

QUALITY	Encouraging, Growing, Learning
CHAKRA	Heart, Solar Plexus
FOCUS	Reframing experiences and thoughts, Embracing fluidity, Compassionate awareness

We are asked to do our best all the time. It's hard to know what that even is when there's no consistent baseline for evaluation. The circles we draw assessing our actions can become tiring, a maze that traps us in the mind.

How do we know when we haven't managed to do our best? Should we do better, can we do better? Peridot elevates our consciousness to see that our best is whatever we actually do in the moment with whatever tools we have at our disposal. It shifts, just as we shift, just as our tools shift. We are forever learning and growing from our experiences.

Appreciate how each moment is completely unique unto itself. Are you still expecting a higher standard from a situation in the past? Peridot empowers us to accept the situation and our actions as they come, to move on with fresh awareness. We can take a moment to reflect and then we must be ready for the present.

Reframe thoughts and experiences with Peridot in:
• Compassion grid (see page 106)
• Love notes (see page 78)

Need a fresh perspective? Go to Green Opal, page 55
Embrace the present with Sodalite, page 45

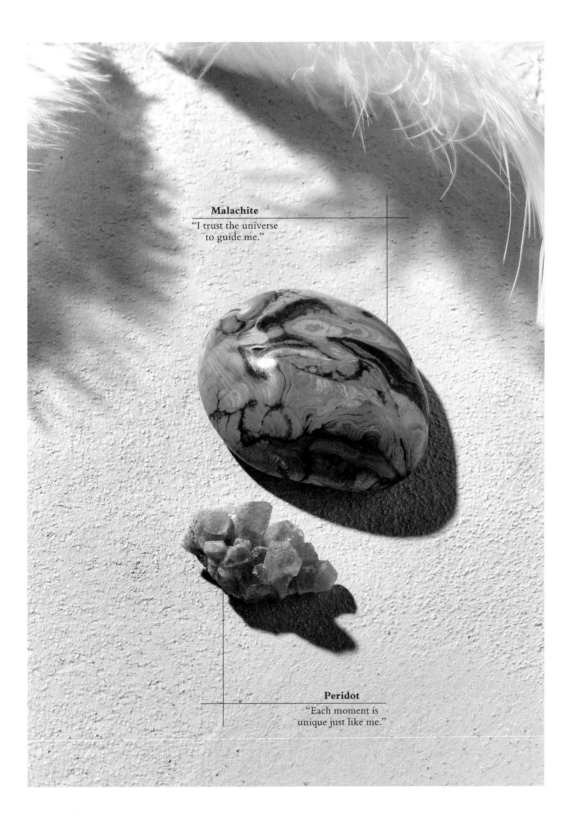

Malachite
"I trust the universe to guide me."

Peridot
"Each moment is unique just like me."

Rutile

"I move between
time and space open
to divine guidance."

Dalmantine

"I see where I am as
the perfect place for
me to be."

Rutile

Present, Mysterious, Perceptive | QUALITY
Crown, Third Eye | CHAKRA
Living in the moment, Moving on from past | FOCUS
experiences, Receiving divine downloads

The threads of time – past, present, future – teach us so much about the mystery of life. They challenge us to move beyond and think more critically, opening our perception to see the connections between all things throughout time and throughout space. If we become attached to the memory, lost in the dream, or lack the imagination of possibility we create an imbalance that disrupts our energetic flow.

Anytime we are out of touch with the tenses of life, Rutile reins our vibration back in to help us appreciate the transition of time. We learn to honour the mystery of the moment, and to create space for time to breathe.

Explore your relationship to time. Are you stuck in one tense or out of touch with another? Let your awareness be fluid, flowing between past, present, and future effortlessly. Channel Rutile's energy to gain a glimpse of where you are closed off to the possibilities. Let it transmit the divine messages of how to live in the now and bring your desires into being.

Open up to the possibilities with Rutile in:
• Sunrise or sunset meditation (see page 31)
• Ritual bath (see page 182)

Increase your frequency with Lemurian Seed, page 227
Go deeper into mystery with Stilbite, page 223

Dalmantine

Playful, Curious, Supportive | QUALITY
Root, Crown | CHAKRA
Growing from curiosity, Releasing fear, | FOCUS
Deepening trust

Life happens moment by moment, a constant movement of energy ushering us from one experience to the next. Fear and worry may make us believe that things are not moving so smoothly. The pace and rhythm, however, are divinely aligned for wherever we are.

It can be frustrating to feel stuck and slow or to be moving too fast and thrust beyond our comfort zone. Yet, this is where the heart releases and finds clarity. Dalmantine shows us that each moment prepares us for what's ahead. It gives us space to see how it all comes together perfectly.

Begin to play with life, embracing the moments like old friends that bring out the best in you. How does that shift your frustration and fear? Dalmantine keeps you from jumping ahead and getting stuck in your mind. Let it challenge you to grow from curiosity, to go with the flow of life instead of against it, to discover the view without needing to know where you're headed.

Bring yourself back into alignment with Dalmantine in:
• Cloud watching (see page 52)
• Gardening with stones (see page 52)

Curious? Jump to Chrysanthemum Stone, page 140
Out of touch? Feel your way to Red Calcite, page 35

Epidote

"I am supported by the
universe, there is nothing
holding me back."

Rhodonite

"I accept myself for
everything I am."

Epidote

The feeling of security encourages us to take risks and follow our dreams. We feel capable and resilient, and willing to experience the challenges that are a part of the manifestation process. A slight shake of our foundations, however, can upset our confidence and paralyse our actions.

Being disconnected from what allows us to feel supported and safe diminishes our creative energy. We lose touch with our desires and struggle to bring them into reality. With Epidote's guidance, our vibration resonates on the same wavelength as our desires. Our fears disappear under its support and our dreams revive.

Imagine the universe holding you, ensuring that no matter what happens you are secure. What dream would you bring to life? If you are not already living that dream, find supportive

Supportive, Resonant, Actualizing	QUALITY
Root, Solar Plexus, Heart	CHAKRA
Bringing dreams to life, Finding our foundations, Moving forward after setbacks	FOCUS

inspiration in Epidote. Feel the courage rise and your trust deepen as you begin to manifest your desire.

Use Epidote as often as you need whenever the foundation feels rocky in:
• Wishing ritual (see page 79)
• Gratitude practice (see page 78)

Feeling harmonious? Head to Celestite, page 209
Discover your desires with Magnetite, page 55

Rhodonite

We are encouraged to value only those who believe and view life the same way we do. Cliquing and pushing away any thoughts that challenge our beliefs, we rally around the similarities and reject those who have a different opinion from our own.

It's easy to forget that radical, life-altering ideas often go against the grain. Innovation occurs when we open the forum to ideas beyond those already accepted. Rhodonite encourages us to be open to the expressions of self that do not fit into the norm. It supports us in sharing the wild ideas, asking the uncomfortable questions, and pushing the envelope past what is societally accepted so that change can occur.

Take a chance to bring someone in to share another view, recognizing that it is through the collaboration of our individuality that brilliance

Revolutionary, Radical, Authentic	QUALITY
Heart, Solar Plexus, Throat	CHAKRA
Changing old paradigms, Radical self-acceptance, Welcoming different perspectives	FOCUS

is born. Rhodonite proves we can come together in a different way, helping us open our hearts and minds to see perspectives beyond our own, and inviting in an opportunity for life to shift.

Uncover radical acceptance with Rhodonite in:
• Breathwork (see page 156)
• Heart flow (see page 31)

Open to new ideas? Jump to Gold, page 119
Tunnel vision? Expand with Dendritic Agate, page 22

Eudialyte

QUALITY | Magical, Reviving, Vibrant
CHAKRA | Root, Solar Plexus, Heart
FOCUS | Connecting to our divinity, Balancing energy, Increasing self-compassion

When we examine ourselves, each speck and flaw becomes larger and more pronounced. These fuel emotional narratives that distort the view we have of ourselves and of life. Under such critical inspection the brightness of our spirit quiets and we lose our vibrancy.

Regaining perspective when all that is visible are the imperfections requires immense tenderness. Eudialyte repairs the emotional body to reinvigorate and unify our life force with love. We find our centre again and recalibrate on a soul level, which allows us to see ourselves more compassionately.

Bring balance to your inner and outer experience by appreciating your divine essence. What does it feel like to remember your own magnificence? Eudialyte reminds us that we are a unique expression of the divine. Everything about us is magic.

Soften the tension with Eudialyte in:
- Ritual building
- Love notes (see page 78)

Feeling magical? Go to Indigo Gabbro, page 241
Find your shine with Labradorite, page 219

Pink Tourmaline

QUALITY | Compassionate, Loving, Kind
CHAKRA | Heart
FOCUS | Developing self-love, Soothing anxiety, Healing wounds of the heart

Our hearts are hungry for loving connection, an experience that lowers stress and soothes the soul. The desire for love can create imbalance if we focus our love only towards other people in our lives, forgetting that love must also be turned inward towards the self.

When we perceive others as perfect without flaws, yet see ourselves unworthy of the same gaze, we distort the energy of love. Pink Tourmaline's energy is a magic mirror that allows us to see ourselves as we truly are – deserving of love. It heals the wounds that make us feel otherwise.

Look at yourself in the mirror. Is your gaze one of love and compassion? Let the calming vibration of Pink Tourmaline soften your critical eye and guide your focus away from the surface imperfections into the deeper layers of the soul. The beauty of you that has been there the whole time now comes into focus.

Cultivate a loving gaze of self-compassion with Pink Tourmaline in:
- Love notes (see page 78)
- Mirror gazing (see page 79)

Feeling the love? Head to Blue Calcite, page 192
Imbalanced heart? Get help from Smithsonite, page 195

Eudialyte
"I am divine, I am magic."

Pink Tourmaline
"I am worthy."

Pegmatite

QUALITY	Empowering, Mystical, Dynamic
CHAKRA	Heart, Crown
FOCUS	Embracing divinity, Lifting the spirit, Finding energetic equilibrium

We are mythical beings always connected to spirit, but day-to-day responsibilities tend to distract us from our divinity. They keep us contained and focused on the physical realm. How then do we reclaim that connection to the spiritual while living in the material world?

We may look for a quick answer from outside ourselves, avoiding the opportunity to reflect on what we do and why. Pegmatite lifts our spirits out of the mundane, enabling us to witness the potential we have in making the world a more magical and loving place. It encourages us to think more deeply about our intentions, recognizing how our relationship to the mundane serves as metaphor for our relationship to the divine.

Allow the energy behind your intentions to create meaning in every action, elevating it from routine obligation to ritual offering. Can you see the divine more clearly now? The energy of Pegmatite gives us the ability to move between physical and spiritual experience, shifting our perception so we begin to recognize the divinity in everything.

Uplift your soul with Pegmatite in:

- Stargazing (see page 52)
- Divine light meditation (see page 157)
- Love notes (see page 78)

Seeing the divine? Open up to Morganite, page 228

Find ritual support with Ammonite, page 21

Austinite

Expansive, Flexible, Courageous	**QUALITY**
Crown, Third Eye	**CHAKRA**
Welcoming new ideas, Expanding belief systems, Softening the ego	**FOCUS**

Stagnant beliefs keep our perception of the world oblivious to the shades between the binary. We hold onto them fearing the change that comes when we waver from the status quo. The trouble is, our world is ever changing and our beliefs must be flexible in order to assimilate the new revelations that appear daily.

Whenever our beliefs are contradicted, it feels like a personal attack. Austinite softens the reception, enabling us to see where there is room for our beliefs to evolve and expand. As life flows, more information becomes available, and what we were not aware of before now enters our consciousness.

As your beliefs are challenged, do you stubbornly refuse to consider the new perspective? Austinite gives us the courage and vulnerability to see where our beliefs fall short.

In doing so, we have the opportunity to open our hearts to new thoughts and possibilities that empower the world to grow.

Keep going deeper with Austinite in:
- Sense writing (see page 212)
- Serene silence (see page 238)

For courage jump to Green Aventurine page 28
Afraid of change? Turn to Phantom Quartz, page 233

Thulite

Infinite, Releasing, Appreciative	**QUALITY**
Heart, Crown	**CHAKRA**
Understanding our priorities, Connecting to the infinite energy of the universe	**FOCUS**

We base our life around time, becoming so wrapped up in it and the way it defines us. The ticking clock creates internal pressure, reminding us how far along we are and how much more there is to do. We lose all sense of our self-worth, attributing it to what we produce by when.

Focusing on time takes up energetic space, the space to feel and find our flow. If we are always rushing to get somewhere, always rushing to achieve, we miss the life that we are living. Under Thulite's energy, we are empowered to redefine our relationship to time, recognizing that it is a construct of society. Thulite teaches us that life is sweet and it's the joy and love that make it so, not the output of each moment.

Reimagine your life outside of time. Imagine your spirit as endless. With Thulite's energy by your side, try tapping into the infinite quality of the universe, detaching your self-worth from time. Let it show you how to stop and appreciate the moment. Let it help you see the beauty you keep passing by.

Find a slower pace with Thulite in:
- Crystal yin yoga (see page 134)
- Gratitude practice (see page 78)

Tap into life's sweetness with Blue Apatite, page 199
Visualize a new way of being with K2 Stone, page 203

See images on pages 98–99

Serandite

QUALITY	Harmonious, Clarifying, Expressive
CHAKRA	Throat, Heart
FOCUS	Heart-centred communication, Showing love with actions, Being vulnerable

Pegmatite
"I move freely between heaven and earth."

Each of our voices is unique, as if we speak a language all our own. Misunderstandings are bound to occur with the expectation that everyone conform to our expression. How do we clear the confusion and connect when it seems we all speak differently?

It may be difficult and uncomfortable to connect when it feels like there are so many obstacles to being understood. Serandite shows that communication is not limited to words but embodies actions and intentions too. Patience, practice, and vulnerability are the tools to use and Serandite teaches us how to use them.

How's your energetic dialogue? Employ the communication tools Serandite shares to create more respect and understanding in your conversations. Harmony comes when we are able to listen with our body, mind, and soul and communicate with people heart to heart.

Open up to more vulnerable expression with Serandite in:
• Hand-holding meditation (see page 157)
• Reiki (see page 182)

Serandite
"I communicate with my body, mind, and soul."

Communication blues? Go to Cuprite, page 65
Embrace your unique voice with Brookite, page 66

Austinite
"I welcome fresh perspectives."

Thulite
"I live life with full presence."

Rhodolite

"My heart keeps me
centred and balanced."

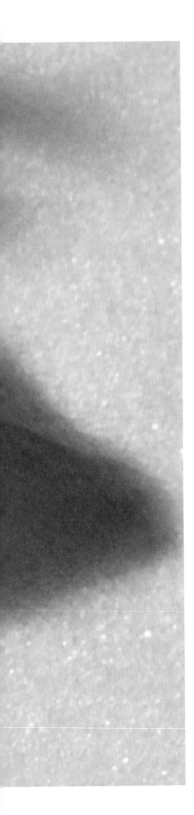

Rhodolite

Balancing, Resilient, Enthusiastic	**QUALITY**
Root, Heart	**CHAKRA**
Finding your centre, Accepting perpetual imperfection, Cultivating resilience	**FOCUS**

Balance is a constant juggling act. We are always shifting the weight around finding our centre, finding our footing, aligning ourselves to our heart. The result is worth it – a lightness in being, grace, and the ability to stand tall.

We don't arrive at this balanced state perfectly and we never will. Rhodolite manages our expectations by showing us that balance is the ability to be flexible and find stability even when our foundation is wobbly. It keeps us from feeling discouraged if we fall down, encouraging us to get right back up and try again.

When life throws something unexpected your way, Rhodolite helps you find balance through the heart. Let your practice, whatever form that takes, keep your energy supple. The lightness of being that follows is its own reward.

Embrace the process with Rhodolite in:

- Chakra balancing (see page 156)
- Heart flow (see page 31)

AIR

Off balance? Find it with Tiger's Eye, page 121
Feeling light? Turn to Kunzite, page 215

Creedite

QUALITY | Inclusive, Intentional, Communicative
CHAKRA | Throat, Heart, Third Eye
FOCUS | Intentional expression, Deep listening, Comfort with silence

We rush to be the first to speak, we keep speaking until we have the last word. We forget to honour the silence in between, to let our expression breathe. Our language loses its substance when we don't express it intentionally, or when we forget the art of listening.

It is in the pause where we give everything within us time to align so our words are heard fully, their meaning and intention surfacing. The pause creates space for others to be heard too. Creedite facilitates more intentional expression by keeping us in our integrity. Our ego softens under its guidance and we feel comfortable with the quiet space in conversation. Wisdom comes from the silence, not the speech.

Can you give yourself a moment between your words to allow your expression the space to resonate? Can you be conscious of what you are saying and why? Creedite helps us communicate from the heart and reminds us to pause so the container generated by our expression can facilitate deeper connection and reflection.

Use Creedite to cultivate space in communication in:
- Serene silence (see page 238)
- Reiki (see page 182)

Deepen intention with Tanzanite, page 191
Need a cleansing breath? Turn to Charoite, page 200

Crazy Lace Agate

QUALITY | Surprise, Resilient, Delightful
CHAKRA | All
FOCUS | Embracing uncertainty, Exploring the unknown, Doing things differently

Every which way life flows, the story unfolds. It can seem chaotic, unpredictable, uncertain, and it is! We hold life so dear that these erratic movements can leave us feeling out of sorts and off-balance. Our conditioned response is to hold on tighter, but the more firm our grasp, the less we feel in control.

The constant surprise of life ensures opportunities have the possibility to arrive. Crazy Lace Agate opens us up to this exploration of energy, where we learn to welcome whatever comes with arms opened wide. It empowers us to break free of the conditioning, to do life our own way. Its wild form reminds us not to take everything so seriously.

Embrace this wild flow that lets you grow through the trials and errors. Can you let the story unfold without curating every page? What parts of you are feeling constrained by your conditioning? Crazy Lace Agate gives you permission to be yourself, to do things differently. Feel the liberation that comes when you respect life's strength. Find the way to loosen your grip and learn to laugh off chaos. While our precious life may seem delicate, it is also robust and resilient. We are meant to live life to the fullest!

Welcome in the wildness with Crazy Lace Agate in:
- Creativity grid (see page 106)
- Breathwork (see page 156)

Experience delight, turn to Fairy Stone, page 211
Cool the chaos with Stibnite, page 150

Crazy Lace Agate
"I enjoy the wild ride of life."

Creedite
"There is room for all words to be heard."

Dioptase

"My feelings help me
learn and grow, in them
I find peace."

Ruby in Zoisite

"The universe helps
me through whatever
challenges come my way."

Ruby in Zoisite

Empowering, Loving, Grounding | **QUALITY**
Root, Heart, Crown | **CHAKRA**
Releasing trauma, Self-love, | **FOCUS**
Discovering universal support

Grounding through the heart helps us come home to ourselves. We see the deeper connections that link us, the deeper love that connects all our hearts. Love as a vibration strengthens the energetic body to release grief, supporting spiritual development from a place of deep self-awareness.

When we feel held by something greater than ourselves we can step away from letting limiting beliefs dictate the possibilities our life can take. Ruby in Zoisite holds our hands through this realization. It encourages us to let it all out by providing a safe space in which we feel comfortable and capable of release. Tapped into it we transcend the barriers that make it difficult to love ourselves deeply.

Connect to the ground beneath you. Lean into love. How does the connection between the Earth and your heart empower you? With Ruby in Zoisite, we know that the only way out is through. We are given the courage to move forward with its reminder that the universe is supporting us.

Find your way through with Ruby in Zoisite in:
- Stones on the body (see page 30)
- Breathwork (see page 156)

Empowered? Go deeper with Smoky Quartz, page 54
Lean into love with Green Aventurine, page 28

Dioptase

Fearless, Peaceful, Guiding | **QUALITY**
Sacral, Throat | **CHAKRA**
Laughing it off, Embracing impermanence, | **FOCUS**
Working through fear

Fear is a big feeling. One that can keep us from truly experiencing life fully. It dampens our desires and crushes the possibilities. Yet respecting the wisdom it offers allows us to transform fear into an expression of courage.

We cannot avoid fear or the discomfort it brings. We must navigate the tough stuff to find our way to love. Dioptase shows us how to use our fear to discover our deeper feelings and connect with greater vulnerability. Peace follows whenever we are open to learning from our discomfort.

Remember your resilience and invite a sense of playfulness into your energetic repertoire. Can you let yourself be free to laugh and shake all the heaviness off? What happens when you meet each challenge with a burst of laughter? Dioptase's energy is an invitation to release the pressure, initiating the transformation of fear so long as we are willing to explore it. With its bold vibration by our side, we learn how to lean into the moment and make it through even the most tumultuous of situations with fortitude.

Find strength in your fear with Dioptase in:
- Breathwork (see page 156)
- Sense writing (see page 212)

Already playful? Flip to Green Apophyllite, page 22
Find peace with support from River Rock, page 41

Guidance through grids

Crystal grids are a wonderful way to channel divine wisdom to receive the information and inspiration that can help us figure out the next step. Use the grids below anytime you're looking for answers, desire more clarity, or are unsure of how to move forward.

Creativity grid

The creative flow can easily be interrupted by a number of different influences. No matter which stage of the process you are in, find your flow by closing your eyes and taking a few deep breaths to channel your creative energy. Each breath deepens your awareness, guiding the supportive elements to the surface of your mind. When you feel them rising, open your eyes and place five stones in a circle, and another stone in the middle. The centre stone represents your creative flow or project, the bottom two represent the supportive energies to work with, the side stones are how to handle distractions, and the top stone is the energetic essence that allows you to know you are on track. Decipher their wisdom by exploring the entries in this book.

Compassion grid

There are moments when our hearts have hardened towards the world. We are quick to judge, impatient with ourselves and each other, and struggle to feel joy. Find softness again by breathing in deep to centre your energy, reflecting on where and how compassion has been missing from your life. Once aware of those areas, place a stone directly in front of you to represent your heart and its wound, with another four guard stones to create a protective box around the heart stone. Place a final stone anywhere outside the box, indicating what you wish could make it through. The guard stones offer direction on how and where you can open up in life to receive what the heart desires and heal its wound.

Moon phase grid

The phases of the moon carry their own special wisdom and guidance. Channel crystalline insight by setting an intention and creating a circle of eight stones, one for each phase of the moon, flowing anticlockwise with the New Moon on the top, followed by Waxing Crescent, First Quarter, Waxing Gibbous, Full Moon, Waning Gibbous, Last Quarter, and finally Waning Crescent. Each crystal represents the energy to cultivate or work with during that specific moon phase in support of your intention. There's no need to wait for a fresh cycle - start wherever you are.

Clockwise from top: **Kunzite** page 215, **Scolecite** page 84, **Purple Fluorite** page 167, **Blue Kyanite** page 185, **Lemurian Seed Quartz** page 227, **Yellow Fluorite** page 119, **Tangerine Quartz** page 129, **Golden Apatite** page 38, **Amazonite** page 75, **Amethyst Flower** (centre) page 215

Wulfenite
"I see myself with eyes of love."

Wulfenite

QUALITY	Liberating, Wild, Shining
CHAKRA	Solar Plexus, Heart
FOCUS	Embracing individuality, Developing confidence, Finding our unique voice

When all eyes are upon us evaluating our essence we begin to shrink. We are afraid of being seen and possibly rejected. It's easier to project a version of who we are. But in the end, we feel alone, our spirit never getting a chance to shine.

We assume it's our likability that matters instead of our truth and alter ourselves to fit into the tiny container of society's acceptance. Whenever we try to tame our spirit Wulfenite brings us back into ourselves and cultivates the ability to stand confidently as we are. It liberates our spirit from needing the approval of others to survive, guiding us to the magic places and people who appreciate us for us.

Who are you when no one is around? Do you shift yourself in the presence of others? Wulfenite wakes up our wildness, encouraging us to appreciate all the qualities that are the unique expression of ourselves. With its liberating vibration, no matter the circumstances, you'll feel confident to shine, to let your beautiful, wild self be seen.

Let loose your wild side with Wulfenite in:
• Mirror gazing (see page 79)
• Chakra balancing (see page 156)

People pleasing? See Blue Tiger's Eye, page 68
Ready to be seen? Open up to Amazonite, page 75

Pink Opal

Soothing, Freeing, Nurturing   **QUALITY**
Heart, Crown   **CHAKRA**
Finding compassionate environments for healing,   **FOCUS**
Releasing inner tensions, Listening to our hearts

There's a reason we all crave peaceful spaces. The tranquility we find there is incredibly healing, it is where the quietest stirrings of the heart can be heard. When life becomes intense, tranquility has a soothing effect on the emotional body, restoring and calming our vibration.

For those moments where the weight of the world feels too heavy, Pink Opal becomes our sacred space. It prompts us to identify where and how serenity lives in our bodies. Supported by its soothing energy we are able to think, feel, calm, and heal. We energetically realign to our heart centre.

Find yourself in the most simple form, nurtured by Pink Opal's pure compassion. What messages of the heart can you hear being whispered? Let its tranquil energy be your cloud, the soft landing, the safe space, the pure acceptance that welcomes stillness and the reflections that follow. Take a deep breath as it soothes all the worries within and releases the tension you've held for so long. Hear it sing to you the reminder that you are free.

Pink Opal helps you find tranquility in:
- Reiki (see page 182)
- Mineral nap (see page 182)
- Water meditation (see page 182)

AIR

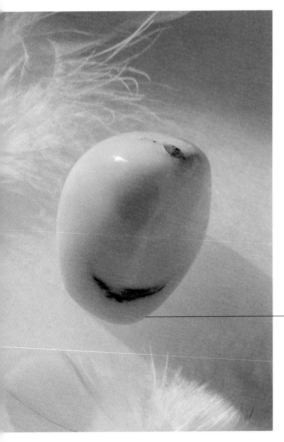

Pink Opal

"My tranquil mind
amplifies the messages
of my heart."

Emotionally tight? See Aquamarine, page 160
Cultivate self-acceptance with Rose Quartz, page 176

Soapstone

QUALITY	Adventurous, Innovative, Adaptable
CHAKRA	Sacral, Solar Plexus, Heart
FOCUS	Breaking free from the plan, Releasing the need to be prepared, Remaining open to possibility

We love to rationalize, plan, and project. Anticipating what could happen gives us a sense of control. There are endless things to worry about and we delay our actions until we all have the details in place. The research takes a lot of energy and we hardly ever feel prepared for what we encounter.

Our desire for everything to be just so forces life into a box. We need the surprises of life to challenge us - if everything went according to plan, we would never learn or grow. Soapstone is the supportive base that helps us embrace unexpected transitions. It keeps the magic of possibility alive, by reminding us it's often more fun when we allow space for spontaneity.

Look at the possibilities. Channel Soapstone's adventurous energy to see the opportunity for expanded delight in breaking free from the plan. Remember Soapstone's deeper message that you are always exactly where you should be and any space we leave for the unexpected invites magic to occur.

Embrace the unexpected adventure with Soapstone in:
• Serene silence (see page 238)
• Walking meditation (see page 30)

Soapstone

"My creative energy guides me towards expansive possibilities."

Ready to go? Head to Moldavite, page 122

Still worried about the future? See Sodalite, page 45

Datolite

"All the information
I need is inside me."

Datolite

Respectful, Informative, Wise	QUALITY
Third Eye, Sacral	CHAKRA
Seeing things for what they are, Thoughtful observation, Honouring the experience	FOCUS

Emotions clouded by the ego have a way of warping the mind. They shift our perspective so we see things as we imagined them occurring or want them to be, not as they truly are. We cannot learn from life if we remain ignorant to reality. We will keep encountering the barriers impeding us from receiving clarity or honest connection.

If we find ourselves stuck in feeling things through the ego, we may feel victimized by our experiences and lack the motivation to engage with compassion and vulnerability. Datolite helps us receive the wisdom in our experiences and detach from the ego so we can work with the information we receive impartially.

Honour your experiences. Let your heart see them from a neutral vantage point. Can you feel your understanding of truth deepen? Datolite's respectful vibration empowers us to be more thoughtful, open, and confident with our reflections and in our relationships. We learn how to reframe our experiences for spiritual growth without letting the ego or emotions take the lead.

Embrace Datolite's informative perspective in:
• Crystal contemplation (see page 213)
• Sunrise or sunset meditation (see page 31)

Shift your perspective with Desert Rose, page 29
Reframe your experiences with Chiastolite, page 62

Shattuckite

QUALITY	Resourceful, Aware, Collaborative
CHAKRA	Sacral, Heart, Third Eye
FOCUS	Reshaping reality, Channelling messages, Amplifying energetic intentions

The universe is always listening. It picks up the subtle expressions of our deepest feelings and desires, creating the situations that will lead us to them. Yet for all this divine intervention, we are still asked to participate in their manifestation.

The realization of our dreams requires space for them to be nurtured and grow. Our hesitation comes when we are holding onto something of the past that needs to be let go. Shattuckite loosens our grip of what used to define our reality, offering instead expansive possibility. It reminds us to play our part in creating space for what's ahead.

Explore the way you co-create with the universe. Are you willing to do your fair share of the work? Evaluate what you are holding onto and let Shattuckite help channel the divine messages that tell you whether to keep something or if it is time to let go. If we follow the guidance, we will make room for our dreams and know the next steps to bring them to life.

Shattuckite's conscious vibration helps manifest dreams into reality in:
• Wishing ritual (see page 79)
• Moon phase grid (see page 106)

Make changes with Rainbow Moonstone, page 171
Co-create with the universe with Malachite, page 88

THE CRYSTALS

Shattuckite

"My thoughts create
my reality."

Citrine

"I release the need to be perfect, I am enough."

Citrine

It is easy to get caught up in the manifestation of our dreams. We envision them as if they've already arrived, forgetting to participate in the process. The action requires us to be confidently decisive. Not an easy request with the endless options at our fingertips, or the pressure for each step to be perfect.

If our focus gets caught on the end product, we may encounter difficulty with knowing how to move forwards. Citrine reminds us that our motivation and dedication illuminate the path ahead and highlight the next steps. It addresses the roots of procrastination, reminding us that taking action is more important than perfection.

Our action paralysed with fear will be incorrect or not enough. Citrine helps us release the need to be perfect and opens us up to the exploration our progress offers. When we accept

Clear, Motivated, Creative	QUALITY
Solar Plexus, Crown	CHAKRA
Moving the dream into reality, Acting on the next steps, Releasing the need for perfection	FOCUS

that we are always learning, always growing, we stay on track and see the possibility in everything.

Activate this energy with Citrine any time you want to move forwards and bring something into fruition with:

• Creativity grid (see page 106)
• Divine light meditation (see page 157)

Release perfectionism with Black Moonstone, page 195
On track? Keep going with Snowflake Obsidian, page 27

Amber

We want it now and are not willing to wait. In our rush, we overlook the red flags indicating our desire is out of alignment. Moving forwards with intention and awareness can be tricky when emotions cloud the process and the pace.

Adhering to divine timing takes courage and trust. If we are willing to listen, we pick up on all the wisdom from the past that is here to guide us. Amber slows our speed, connecting us to the intention behind our actions and desires. We become better collaborators with the universe with its support.

Where in life are you rushing? Take a deeper look within while asking yourself, "Am I doing this to keep up with the people around me or am I moving forwards because it's the right thing to do?" When we are clear on the intention, Amber helps us find our own pace towards manifestation.

Absorbing, Patient, Thoughtful	QUALITY
Solar Plexus, Root, Heart	CHAKRA
Releasing urgency, Moving forwards in alignment with our desires, Listening to divine timing	FOCUS

Channel the energy of Amber whenever you lose sight of internal wisdom and are trying to rush ahead, with:

• Cloud watching (see page 52)
• Crystal reading (see page 212)

Running on divine time? See Fairy Stone, page 211
Trying to keep up with others? See Girasol, page 165

See image on page 117

Fire Opal

QUALITY	Cosmic, Ethereal, Transcending
CHAKRA	Solar Plexus, Sacral, Third Eye, Crown
FOCUS	Spiritual illumination, Witnessing magic in action, Feeling the whisper of the divine

The universe often asks us to believe in the most impossible of things. Each day we are challenged to remain open and receptive to its magic. For some of us, it's much easier to focus on the explanations instead of embracing the ethereal expressions of the divine.

The curiosity to know more and to know why can be beautiful. However, too much logic and reasoning can make anything lose its lustre. Fire Opal is a gift of transcendence. It directly connects us to ethereal source vibrations that whisper wisdom into our beings. We see its flicker, and we see magic in action – illuminating, activating, and inspiring us to believe in the wild, unimaginable possibilities.

If you're struggling to see life's shimmer, let Fire Opal rekindle your awareness of magic by cultivating a deeper appreciation for the interconnectedness of life around you. All the ideas are held in one, and as our perspective shifts we are awakened to something completely different, new, unreal. We get to choose how far to take the dream. We get to decide in the end what makes it into the world.

Engage with Fire Opal's eye-opening energy whenever you lose touch with the magic of now in:
- Stargazing (see page 52)
- Forest bathing (see page 52)
- Crystal contemplation (see page 213)

Seeing magic? Go further with Indigo Gabbro, page 241

Lost in logic? Break free with Coral, page 175

Carnelian

QUALITY	Courageous, Passionate, Bold
CHAKRA	Root, Sacral, Solar Plexus
FOCUS	Creating from within, Remembering what it feels like to be alive, Moving through fear

We're taught to follow all the rules, to be like everybody else. Our creative fire is restricted by a world built around fear. It's not easy remembering the brilliance that swirls inside, and it's even more challenging to find the courage to express it.

Each of us is unique. Life is the opportunity to let our individuality shine. Carnelian activates the courage within to be who we are. It invigorates us to try when we are full of fear or worry. It reminds us that our mistakes are beautiful training grounds for innovation. Breathe deeply, noting where you feel tightness in the body. What are

you holding there and how is it holding you back? Is there a fear hiding there?

Carnelian reconnects us to our inner pioneer teaching us how to boldly follow our own lead. When we are OK doing things differently the possibilities open up more fully.

Whenever hesitation creeps in, channel Carnelian for a power boost in:
- Breathwork (see page 156)
- Hand-holding meditation (see page 157)
- Stones on the body (see page 30)

Feeling bold? Get louder with Moss Agate, page 46

Still shy? See your beauty with Jacaré Quartz, page 80

Fire Opal

"I see the magic in all things everywhere."

Amber

"The universe guides me to be in the right place at the right time."

Carnelian

"Whenever fear or doubt crosses my mind, I remember that my heart beats with pure courage."

Honey Calcite

QUALITY	Energizing, Empowering, Harmonious
CHAKRA	Solar Plexus, Heart
FOCUS	Happiness through liberation, Seeing the effect of our actions, Living in integrity

There's a huge energetic shift coming, one focused not around society's standards, but on our own energetic integrity. We see the hopes and dreams for the future connected to the transformation of society.

Our purpose is linked to liberation. Our happiness is tied to equality. Under Honey Calcite's empowering energy we balance sweetness with radical truth, we see our actions as direct reflections of our values. It is a call to action, showing us what is needed to bring peace, harmony, and liberation into the world.

Whenever we find ourselves complacent, Honey Calcite shines brightly, illuminating us all the way through and opening us up to a new way of being. It encourages us to take a deeper look at how our energy is rippling out creating the waves that determine the shoreline – only this shoreline is a new paradigm. Ask yourself, "What am I willing to do if I knew it would bring peace into the world tomorrow?" and then get to it!

Bring radical truth into your actions daily with Honey Calcite in:
- Aura meditation (see page 213)
- The gaze (see page 238)
- Golden channel meditation (see page 238)

For liberation head to Crazy Lace Agate, page 102
See the bigger picture with Desert Jasper, page 36

Yellow Fluorite

Clarity is necessary for us to envision our dreams. It comes from the transformative silence that we find when we are alone with our own vibration. This is the silence that allows us to hear our energetic vibration speak.

Alone with ourselves is an uncomfortable place to be. This is where everything goes quiet and we are left to confront all that we have been running from, conscious or not. Yellow Fluorite is the golden illumination bringing sight to otherwise unseen parts of our soul. Lifted by its energy, we can see our shame from a compassionate perspective, dynamically shifting it into a vibration of empowerment.

Breathe deep and look at yourself in the mirror. Do you love yourself enough to enjoy being alone in your own vibration? Invigorating the heart and soul, Yellow Fluorite elevates you

Invigorating, Deepening, Clearing	QUALITY
Solar Plexus, Sacral, Crown	CHAKRA
Cultivating inner awareness, Hearing the vibrations of our soul, Shifting the dynamic of shame	FOCUS

above fear. It helps you to embrace whatever challenging feelings or memories you find, breathing new life and inspiration in its wake.

Cultivate active stillness with Yellow Fluorite whenever the breath feels shallow. Use it in:
• Serene silence (see page 238)
• Golden channel meditation (see page 238)

_____

Afraid of the silence? Seek out Green Kyanite, page 80
Comfortable? See Clear Apophyllite, page 207

Gold

Strength is often seen as a firm and forceful quality, valued for the way it is impervious to external force. When we embrace this view of strength, we disconnect from source, thinking we are alone in the world and must stand firm. Yet, this "us against the world" mentality always makes us come up short.

Strength is the ability to shift and take on new shape as necessary. The more rigid a substance, the more prone to shattering. Gold embodies strength as a malleable energy that is open and receptive to change.

We are not alone in this world. Every moment we are coming into contact with another expression of universal energy. Follow Gold's lead and learn to appreciate these unique expressions of the world, and shift when necessary. Source energy is ever flowing and constantly shaping us,

Malleable, Morphing, Connected	QUALITY
Solar Plexus, Crown	CHAKRA
Opening up to the influences of the universe, Redefining strength, Embracing change	FOCUS

we don't need to be so afraid of the new form we will take.

If you find yourself rejecting the lessons from the universe let Gold teach you how to find a more flexible approach. Use it in:
• Divine light meditation (see page 157)
• Stones on the body (see page 30)

_____

Want to make a difference? See Grape Agate, page 227
Feel alone? Find community with Amazonite, page 75

See images on pages 120–121

Tiger's Eye

"My energy is aligned with my heart, I always feel centred."

Yellow Fluorite

"My wounds are the creative wells for my deepest inspirations."

Honey Calcite

"My actions mirror my values, each one is an act of liberation and harmony."

Gold

"I am soft and
I am strong."

Tiger's Eye

Aligning, Balancing, Integrating — **QUALITY**

Solar Plexus — **CHAKRA**

Merging the inner and outer expressions of our energy, Healthy prioritization — **FOCUS**

Life is a constant dance between our inner and outer worlds, a delicate balancing act where the extremes must find their centre. As empathetic beings, guilt can often determine our priorities, setting us askew, and leaving us feeling overwhelmed and depleted.

If we are always having others direct our priorities, how will we ever find balance? Tiger's Eye acts as our tethering pole, helping us discover our centre line. It keeps us living in our integrity by bringing all aspects of our vibration in for assessment. We learn to filter life through our core and align it to the heart, enabling us to move forwards with conscious decision, without leaking our energy.

Evaluate your priorities and identify the areas where your guilt overwhelms your decision making. Can you recalibrate keeping your energy aligned so you can direct it intentionally? Under Tiger's Eye we say "no" when we need to and "yes" only when we mean it. With its support we merge the inner and outer essence to authenticate our expression and keep us from falling into people pleasing.

Engage Tiger's Eye anytime you are overwhelmed or overcommitting. Use it in:

• Chakra balancing (see page 156)

• Reiki (see page 182)

• Crystal yin yoga (see page 134)

FIRE

Stop people pleasing with Hematite, page 24

Already balanced? See Stilbite, page 223

Moldavite

QUALITY	Rapid, Open, Transcendent
CHAKRA	Heart
FOCUS	Accelerated spiritual ascension, Surrendering to the universe, Embracing cosmic energy

The spiritual path is a lifelong experience. Every now and again we come up against a situation that leaves us filled with resistance or fear, or both. We've fallen too far down and need an energetic boost.

When we are resistant to change or fearful of the next step, Moldavite is the antidote. The vibration moves us so quickly we do not have time to think twice about holding on. It's an exciting ride and challenges us with its rapid jumps that skip steps and blaze past experiences that provide context. It's for adventurous spirits who are completely surrendering to the universe.

Are you ready to make some big spiritual leaps? Take a trust fall with Moldavite. It's the stone we use when we've got everything and nothing to lose. Be ready to move fast and be prepared to arrive delightfully disoriented. Moldavite is the catalyst that brings us out of the paradigm back into the ether of love. No looking back.

Work with Moldavite energy when you are looking for a complete energetic upgrade in:
- Breathwork (see page 156)
- Stones on the body (see page 30)

Ready for next level? See Gwindel Quartz, page 220
Still unsure? Get ready with Prehnite, page 68

Snakeskin Agate

QUALITY	Transforming, Vulnerable, Curious
CHAKRA	Sacral, Solar Plexus
FOCUS	Moving beyond your comfort zone, Getting out of energetic ruts, Evolving

As we learn life lessons they plump us up with wisdom. When we begin to feel tight, maybe a little stuck, it's time for a change, to move up a level, to release and move on. Sometimes we get comfortable where we are, choosing to feel secure and not realizing we're stagnant.

We cannot grow if we are stuck in the comfort of the past. Staying small prevents our gifts from entering the world. Snakeskin Agate ensures that if we've learned the lessons, we move on and let ourselves be challenged. It stimulates our curiosity for the bigger world and the potential role we could play in it.

Take a deep breath and let go. How does it feel to be undergoing transformation? How does it feel to embrace the tenderness of a new challenge? Snakeskin Agate encourages us to let go of the confines of our hearts and expand to make space within. The first transformation is the strangest, but after that we are ready to do it all over again.

For moments when you're stuck in an energetic rut, Snakeskin Agate's energy can lift you out. Try using it in:
- Breathwork (see page 156)
- Ritual bath (see page 182)

Transforming? Head to Spirit Quartz, page 225
Stuck in your comfort zone? See Sulphur, page 130

Moldavite

"I have full trust in the universe and I'm ready to go wherever it wants to take me."

Snakeskin Agate

"I am endlessly transforming, letting go, and welcoming in new experiences."

Basalt

QUALITY	Fearless, Welcoming, Transforming
CHAKRA	Root, Crown
FOCUS	Embracing impermanence, Releasing attachment, Encouraging energetic flow

The more we hold onto, the more we become locked in the past, inhibiting our progression. It's not that nostalgia or sentiment is wrong, but if we are not able to release them, we lose sight of what follows - our rebirth, the evolutionary process that occurs when our energy is in flow.

The past expression of Basalt is molten lava, which moves slowly over long distances before it cools. It doesn't try to hold onto what it once was, it accepts the transition and in doing so allows its form to become a host to other surprising minerals like like Gold, Mesolite, and Feldspar. We too can gracefully accept our transitions from memory into the moment. Basalt teaches us a lesson in impermanence and the possibilities that are available to us when we are open to movement.

Where are you fearful and resistant to the natural progressions of life? Basalt reminds us that we are safe. Its grounding vibration helps us appreciate and detach so we can undergo our own energetic transformation. As we flow, we open ourselves up to something greater.

Feel Basalt's transformative effects in:
• Stones on the body (see page 30)
• Cloud watching (see page 52)

Basalt

"I embrace the flow of my
energy, allowing room
for transformation."

Ready to move on? Flip to Cinnabar, page 136
Find grace in transitions with Tanzanite, page 191

124

Aragonite

"I let the stars within me shine, there's no need to hide my cosmic energy."

Aragonite

There's the self that we project onto the world, an easier to digest version of ourselves, and the one we keep safe inside for fear that we are too much. Our fear keeps us living small, playing it safe, and accommodating. The possibility of rejection is so strong we'd rather stay within the box instead of put ourselves out there.

It's not easy owning one's power or letting oneself be seen. If there's one key lesson Aragonite teaches, it is to boldly reach out from a place of curiosity. When we do, there's an energetic liberation where we feel connected to our cosmic origins and allow ourselves to shine.

Remember we are all made of the same cosmic material as the stars in the universe. Stars from way back when expanded and contracted repeatedly to bring us into being today. Aragonite expands your vibration past the

Authentic, Confident, Beaming	QUALITY
Solar Plexus, Sacral, Root	CHAKRA
Releasing fear and worry, Expanding past personal limitations, Connecting to the cosmos within	FOCUS

internal barriers that hold you back, connecting you to the cosmos within. In doing so, it helps you find an outlet for your infinite and magical qualities that have been waiting to be released.

Break through the barriers with Aragonite in:
- Stargazing (see page 52)
- Breathwork (see page 156)

Step into your power with Zircon, page 154
Develop confidence with Almandine Garnet, page 38

Pyrite

QUALITY	Empowering, Authentic, Inspiring
CHAKRA	Solar Plexus
FOCUS	Discovering your own sacred geometry, Experiencing energetic brilliance, Developing confidence

Much of life is about learning and discovery - learning what works and what doesn't; discovering ourselves and the gifts we have to offer. Navigating our path amidst a world of people doing just the same can be daunting.

Instead of looking to others for advice on how to increase our worth and success, Pyrite urges us to let our light shine, imparting a natural confidence that guides the way. Witnessing its angled structure emerging out of the crystal matrix, we find inspiration to let our inner gifts shape our expression into a form of sacred geometry. Pause to examine the shape of your energy. Where are you trying to replicate exactly what you've seen or what has been suggested to you? Pyrite encourages us to make space for our talents to emerge organically and guide our way to an innate perfection that arrives spontaneously. Imbued with its glowing energy, we discover that we are not trying to reinvent what has come before, we are finding our own way of expressing what has always been within.

Come to Pyrite whenever you are desiring a reconnection with your own guiding glow with:
• Golden channel meditation (see page 238)
• Creativity grid (see page 106)

Deepen self-acceptance with Rhodonite, page 93
Let your confidence ring with K2 Stone, page 203

Rutilated Quartz

QUALITY	Enlightening, Evolving, Aware
CHAKRA	Crown, Solar Plexus
FOCUS	Spiritual activation, Transforming the everyday into mystical wonder, Finding your place in time and space

Our daily routine condenses down into a few short blocks of existence - mostly it's the same few locations on repeat. Our mind, body, and soul follow suit, repeating the patterns of familiarity - the same thoughts, actions, and beliefs. And then one day a powerful feeling stirs our curiosity. In that moment, we feel the layers of time and all its permutations meet, and experience déjà vu.

This sensation of having already been there before is a magic portal to the incredible interconnectedness of the universe. Rutilated Quartz represents the threads of time and space that crisscross to create the fabric of life. The awareness it brings encourages our spiritual awakening and reminds us that everything is moving, shifting, changing. We may not witness these transitions, but they are happening.

Examine your daily routine. Have you become lost in the repetition? Step into your spirituality under the tutelage of Rutilated Quartz. Listen as it sparks reflection into the otherwise banal experiences of life. Its activating vibration will connect you to the universe in a way you may never have experienced before, opening you up to see the world with mystical awareness.

Activate your spiritual transformation with Rutilated Quartz in:
• Divine light meditation (see page 157)
• Aura meditation (see page 213)

Stir your curiosity with Dendritic Agate, page 22
Open up to source with Heulandite, page 236

Pyrite

"My energy naturally
expresses itself in the
shape of perfection."

Rutilated Quartz

"I am awakened to the
mysteries and magic
of the universe."

Sunstone

"I see the expression of my power as an opportunity to connect more collaboratively with my community."

Tangerine Quartz

"I invite playfulness into my life and it resets my energy."

Sunstone

The power dynamic created by the top-down leadership approach we've been taught to value removes any potential for equality and innovation, as people must competitively climb over each other to rise up in rank. There's little collaboration because the stakes are too high.

Grappling with the effects of seeing everyone as either above or below you weakens your connection to the community. Sunstone's rays of benevolence show us the tremendous difference between leading from the top versus leading from a place of service. It revolutionizes our relationship to power, so our choices and actions are for the highest good of all.

Explore your expression of leadership. Where could you invite in more collaboration, compassion, and love? With Sunstone's encouragement, you learn the benefits of

Benevolent, Encouraging, Spirited	**QUALITY**
Sacral, Solar Plexus	**CHAKRA**
Learning to lead from a place of service, Promoting a healthy relationship to power	**FOCUS**

working together for the greater good. Embrace its warming benevolence and watch your ability to lead be transformed as it clears out the outdated perspectives regarding leadership and power.

Relax your need to control with Sunstone in:
- Serene silence (see page 238)
- Hand-holding meditation (see page 157)

Ready to collaborate? Explore Blue Apatite, page 199
Feeling optimistic? Open up to Moss Agate, page 46

Tangerine Quartz

As children we don't often have the language or tools to process and release our experiences. We hold onto and deal with them in ways that allow us to get by relatively unscathed, or so we think. Sometimes it works and we keep up the practice, at other times we dig a deeper emotional hole.

Regardless of how we managed certain experiences or trauma at the time, Tangerine Quartz brings us back to that moment to reframe our experiences for our own empowerment.

Go deep into the archives of your existence to recall your experiences. Now that you have a greater perspective on the whole, would it be a good idea to revisit and reframe? Tangerine Quartz encourages us to reflect and reset. Let its playful energy lighten the experience and guide you back into the embrace of supportive connection. Take its invitation to reconnect with

Uplifting, Creative, Playful	**QUALITY**
Sacral, Heart	**CHAKRA**
Processing deep trauma, Reconnecting to our inner child, Reframing challenging experiences	**FOCUS**

your inner child as an opportunity to rediscover the well of creative inspiration waiting for you.

Take a trip into the past with Tangerine Quartz whenever you sense that your responses could use reframing, with:
- Breathwork (see page 156)
- Sense writing (see page 212)

Explore your creative side with Vanadinite, page 41
Process the emotions with Hemimorphite, page 179

Sulphur

QUALITY	Purifying, Awakening, Essential
CHAKRA	Solar Plexus
FOCUS	Trusting our senses, Appreciating the complexity of our emotional natures, Awakening our dynamic existence

We are constantly navigating the rapid shifts of life, each twist and turn can feel like we are playing with fire. The volatility of any situation, feeling, or idea can seem dangerous, yet it is these intense, powerful, and dynamic situations that awaken our souls and strength.

Sulphur is a striking and challenging mineral - it represents our inner flame, the part of us that needs loving attention to thrive. Its softness makes it incredibly susceptible to external forces such as water or heat, but when used and cared for with respect, it brings us in touch with the complex inner workings of our emotional nature.

With Sulphur, volatility can feel like a rebirth wherein whatever is disguising your feelings and boundaries is cleared away, creating space for you to exist as you are. Whether that means feeding the fire within because you've been acting small, or calling attention to a flame that is burning out of control, Sulphur teaches you to move dynamically, shifting as necessary to find the space to burn brightly and the harmony to ensure you are not harming in the process

Nurture your inner fire with Sulphur in:
- The gaze (see page 238)
- Breathwork (see page 156)

Awakened soul? Turn to Tektite, page 246
Acting small? See Hematite, page 24

Orange Calcite

QUALITY	Effervescent, Creative, Connecting
CHAKRA	Sacral, Solar Plexus, Heart
FOCUS	Finding innovative solutions, Overcoming challenges, Transforming gloomy emotions

Sometimes life doesn't go our way. We get stuck trying to make something happen only to repeatedly feel blocked. The little challenges that cross our paths can drop us down a notch, leaving us feeling defeated. Our sour moods are contagious and ripple out into our community. It's OK to have a bad day, but sometimes we just need a little boost to move us up and out and back on track.

Like bubbles quickly popping up to the surface, Orange Calcite lifts us higher, giving us an expanded perception. The vantage point lets us see what is on the horizon, giving us something to look forward to and inspiring us to keep our spirits up. It reminds us that we are not alone and encourages us to lean into our communities. Under its enveloping warmth, we remember what makes us feel alive so we don't get lost in gloom. We remember the people who brighten our day and call upon them for support.

Whenever life has you feeling down and out, breathe in Orange Calcite's uplifting vibration. As your view expands, where can you open up to new ideas and different avenues of action? Where can you reach out into your community? Let Orange Calcite's creative energy keep you going and inspire your next steps.

Get a boost from Orange Calcite in:
- Creativity grid (see page 106)
- Crystal contemplation (see page 213)

Effervescent? Keep going with Phenacite, page 245
Stuck in a rut? Head to Blue Topaz, page 180

Sulphur

"Volatility is empowering,
I nurture my inner flame
with love and compassion."

Orange Calcite

"I only need to take a
deep breath to feel my way
through any challenge."

Rhodochrosite

"My energy stands tall, I move with grace and ease connecting with those who are ready to connect with me."

Spinel

"I heal the past, present, and future with my capacity to forgive."

Rhodochrosite

Graceful, Connective, Balancing	QUALITY
Solar Plexus, Heart	CHAKRA
Releasing fears around commitment, Honouring our boundaries	FOCUS

Our lives are built around relationships and on a deep level we all need companionship to survive. Some of us are afraid to get close, some of us are desperate for contact. We spend so much time in one expression or the other that we have lost the ability to stay upright and receptive to those who are ready for sincere connection.

Fear is the biggest challenge we face when cultivating sincere relationships. It bends us out of shape, distorting our perception, making connection more challenging. Rhodochrosite helps us develop respect and understanding towards the expression of love.

When love is what guides us, our energy moves with grace and ease. We are not lunging into partnership out of desperation, nor are we avoiding out of fear. We are strong, vulnerable, receptive, and honour our boundaries. Love is an energetic exchange built around openness and integrity. We are here to love and be loved … and Rhodochrosite shows us the way.

Find and develop your loving posture with Rhodochrosite in:
• Reiki (see page 182)
• Hand-holding meditation (see page 157)

Feeling the love? See Ruby in Zoisite, page 105
Strengthen connection with Dravite, page 246

Spinel

Ancestral, Joyful, Forgiving	QUALITY
All	CHAKRA
Breaking the cycle of trauma, Leaving everything energetically better than we found it	FOCUS

The lived experiences of our ancestors trickle down through our DNA. Energy passed along may not always be so clear, and one little trigger can open us up to immense pain. This isn't all discomfort though, it's our birthright to heal.

These energetic heirlooms offer much wisdom if we can recognize the threads of their influence. Spinel, a stone whose colour ways are as endless as a rainbow's hues, is the explosive joy that breaks the chain, healing past and future through the present moment. It reaches into time and teaches us how to stop the trauma from perpetuating forward by honouring what came before and respecting the imperfect knowledge and action of the past.

Reflect on what your ancestors energetically passed on to you. Where can you witness their efforts with compassion? Spinel shows us how to forgive and cultivate acceptance of ourselves. Its harmonizing vibration helps us to witness and release, ensuring the energetic heirlooms we pass along are treasures for the next generation.

Break the cycle of trauma with Spinel during:
• Serene silence (see page 238)
• Learning about your ancestors

Open to forgiveness? Turn to Chrysoberyl, page 242
Connect to your ancestors with Turquoise, page 46

Radiant body

Our bodies are living crystals, from our bones and DNA to the fascia holding us together. Just as we would care for the stones in our collection, we must care for ourselves. Nurture your crystal body with these massage and stretching techniques, and watch yourself glow.

Crystal yin yoga

Each of our bodies is held together by its own crystalline structure called fascia, which is thought to store emotional memory. This gentle yoga practice releases the fascia to support us in processing those experiences and feelings held within our bodies. The poses, which are held upwards of five minutes and moved through very slowly, help us find the stillness we need. We become more intentional, aware, and appreciative of life.

Create your own crystal yin practice by choosing a handful of your favourite restorative poses. (Some great options include: Corpse Pose, Banana Pose, Supported Reclining Butterfly Pose, Sleeping Swan Pose, and Reclined Spinal Twist.) Begin with a few minutes of a centring crystal meditation using a stone that is calling to you before slowly flowing through the poses. Use whatever props you need to support your body so it can release fully into the pose, holding each one for three to five minutes. Remember to breathe deeply and to let your mind be fluid.

Massage and minerals

We all hold some sort of muscular tension or weakness brought on by the different habits that define our lives and the repetition of certain activities. We can use massage to help relieve the tension and restore circulation. Crystals formed in specific shapes can be used for various massage techniques, adding an extra layer of vibrational therapy. Take this even deeper by researching the chemical composition of the mineral and aligning it to your body's needs.

- A stone shaped as a massage wand is polished, rounded at one or both ends, and has a bit of heft to it making it easy to hold and press into the tight muscles. It is ideal for calves, thighs, and chest or, if practising on another, it can be used on the back.

- Lymph massage, used to move lymph fluid back towards the heart, is best done with a polished, slightly flat stone with wavelike, rounded edges. Slowly and gently move the stone against the body with light pressure towards the different drainage points in the neck, chest, armpit, crux of the elbow, groin, and back of the knee.

- Similar to lymph massage, Facial Gua Sha uses the same type of stones and method, though with lighter strokes. On prepped skin (hydrating mist and facial oil), swipe a polished and flat stone held at a 15-degree angle slowly across the skin, starting from the centre line and working your way out towards the edge of the face. End with a draining stroke that flows from the centre of the chin, up over the ear and down the side of the neck.

- Wand-shaped stones are perfect for energetic sweeping, where you vibrationally clear your aura. Move the wand in quick circular motions all around the body, paying special attention to the head and heart. Great to do whenever you come home or have been around a lot of people or energy and need to recentre.

Acupressure awakening

Based on the traditional Chinese medicine practice of acupuncture, acupressure uses pressure on certain points to release tension, restore circulation, and relax the body. Using a small pointed crystal wand, you can press different points related to your ailment for relief. Use a more rounded point for the face. One to explore is the Yin Tang point located at the midpoint between the eyebrows. Gently press and move the stone in a circular motion to relieve stress and anxiety.

Cinnabar

QUALITY	Enduring, Alchemical, Clearing
CHAKRA	Sacral, Solar Plexus, Crown
FOCUS	Starting fresh, Making it through the tough times, Transforming experiences and emotions

Our responses to the difficult situations we find ourselves in are often less than ideal. How do we make it through in one piece when there always seems to be another challenge around the bend? We barely scratch the surface of one before we are navigating another.

Sometimes all we crave is a fresh start. An opportunity to take what we've learned and what we've experienced and begin anew. Cinnabar supports this endeavour. Its mercurial energy transforms our experiences and emotions by teaching us the process of energetic alchemy. We tap into our innate creative force to strengthen our resolve and open ourselves to divine guidance.

Maybe it has been a particularly difficult month, day, or even year. Let out a big sigh and acknowledge all that you have been through. Remember, if you ever find yourself stuck and needing a change, Cinnabar will clear away any of the emotional debris and activate your resilience, bringing you back to stable ground with a new reserve of endurance.

Empower your vibration with Cinnabar in:
• Breathwork (see page 156)
• Stones on the body (see page 30)

Move forward with Marble, page 187
Find your power with Diamond, page 208

Serpentine

QUALITY	Resourceful, Divine, Awakened
CHAKRA	Root, Sacral, Crown
FOCUS	Kundalini awakening, Living with intention, Finding your way to the divine

Time is fluid and these days with so much going on it's hard to know what time it is or what day we are in. Everything is blending together into one long afternoon. At some point we will need to wake up and embrace reality.

We don't always need to abide by the standard notions of the watch or calendar, but our relationship to time is important. It offers us structure and supports our spiritual evolution. Serpentine slithers in to remind us that every day is a fresh start, an opportunity to begin again. It reveals the activation of possibility when we integrate the reflections from the night before and choose to live our new day consciously awake and inspired.

If time has floated without your conscious presence, shake yourself awake by moving your body as much and as quickly as you can. Where have you been zoning out and what would it feel like to call back in your energy? Serpentine opens our eyes and awakens our kundalini, the energetic coil within that once unravelled leads us to our divinity. We move forward with inspiration and gratitude, aware and optimistic that our energetic consciousness will lead to spiritual ascension.

Uncoil your energy with Serpentine in:
• Breathwork (see page 156)
• Sunrise or sunset meditation (see page 31)

Reconnect to time with Thulite, page 97
Check in with self-care with Blue Calcite, page 192

Cinnabar
"I have the power
within to transform."

Serpentine
"When I live and act with
intention I connect to
the divine."

Bumblebee Jasper

"I am willing to
participate in the
realization of
my dreams."

Yellow Calcite

"With every breath
the belief I have in
myself grows."

Yellow Calcite

Energizing, Responsive, Kinetic	QUALITY
Solar Plexus, Crown	CHAKRA
Facilitating epiphanies, Ability to overcome, Learning to believe in oneself	FOCUS

When we evaluate the tasks ahead, we often get caught up in the excuses of needing more. "If only I had this or that, then I would really be able to achieve my goals" is a common thought that keeps us procrastinating. The truth is, we can do incredible things with whatever we have.

It can be easy to put off the project or delay participation for lack of the "right" supplies, but what we lose in the process is the innovation that the creative challenges provide. Yellow Calcite keeps us in motion to move past procrastination. Its buzzing energy enables us to overcome fear and instils the belief that we can and we will.

Take a look at your to-do and dream list. What items have you been putting off? Yellow Calcite will guide you through to uncover what is really lurking beneath your hesitation. Is it fear keeping you back, or could you benefit from some creative inspiration? Whichever side you fall, Yellow Calcite will help you figure out how to keep moving towards your goals.

Rekindle your innovative flow with Yellow Calcite in:
• Creativity grid (see page 106)
• Crystal reading (see page 212)

Need more illumination? See Copper, page 191
Deepen your self-trust with White Agate, page 189

Bumblebee Jasper

Participatory, Co-creative, Reciprocal	QUALITY
Root, Solar Plexus, Heart	CHAKRA
Connecting with the community, Managing expectations, Sharing abundance	FOCUS

Sure enough there will be a time when whatever we expect doesn't materialize. It's not to say that our expectations are wrong, but we often forget a crucial component – our participation. Stating our desires and dreams is only half the process, we must also show up and be part of the action.

If we say we desire something, we must also act on and towards that desire. With Bumblebee Jasper's gentle reminder we see our role expand and are encouraged to connect and share our abundant wisdom with each other to support in the manifestation process.

Have you been taking more than you give? Have you been sitting back waiting for the universe to do the work? Bumblebee Jasper reorients your energy reminding you to be present and participatory in life. This shift in behaviour is an act of gratitude for the universe's support that calls in even greater abundance. If you notice delays in your dreams becoming reality, it might be time to take a closer look at where your presence is being requested.

Embrace Bumblebee Jasper's energy in:
• Gratitude practice (see page 78)
• Hand-holding meditation (see page 157)

Cultivate presence with Rutile, page 91
Deepen connections with Golden Apatite, page 38

Chrysanthemum Stone

QUALITY	Open, Auspicious, Attentive
CHAKRA	Third Eye
FOCUS	Receiving divine guidance, Slowing down to absorb life's magic, Rediscovering forgotten dreams

THE CRYSTALS

The universe is always communicating with us. Little messages appear in the most unusual of ways, like magical surprises, to stop us in our tracks and open our senses to what it is trying to say. Move too fast and we may miss these gentle whispers from beyond and the incredible guidance they offer.

These messages help us remember our "why" amidst the chaos, bringing us back to our dreams and reinvigorating our zest for life. Opening our inner vision, Chrysanthemum Stone helps us to perceive the magical essences that are all around us. They only take a minute to receive, but if we're not willing to engage, our capacity to find these omens when we are in desperate need fades away.

Pay attention to the signs; they could be anything – running into an old friend, a conversation with a stranger, a flower etched in stone, an animal appearance, or accidentally taking a wrong turn. Chrysanthemum Stone helps us slow down and remain curious enough to appreciate the wild and random omens. These messages come to guide us through life and arrive when we most need their wisdom.

Open your eyes to the magic of the world around you with Chrysanthemum Stone in:
- Walking meditation (see page 30)
- Forest bathing (see page 52)

Tunnel vision? Head to Unakite Jasper, page 232
Rediscover your dreams with Barite, page 244

Spessartine Garnet

The discovery of fire set in motion a chain of events that transformed the world. Its energy, a natural charisma, captivated humanity. Each of us carries this element, and when we follow the energetic expression of fire within ourselves, we find our creative life force and inner light.

Much like the fire from millions of years past, the discovery of fire within us transforms our whole energetic expression. We can finally appreciate our magnetic qualities that draw in our desires. Spessartine Garnet enhances this ability, channelling our essence towards a specific goal. We find our unique route to abundance, illuminated directly by our internal flame.

Tap into your natural charisma and watch it galvanize your magnetism. How does it influence your ability to take action and manifest? Channel Spessartine Garnet's vibration to inspire further

Illuminating, Activating, Magnetic	QUALITY
Root, Sacral	CHAKRA
Drawing in abundance, Embracing the fire within, Developing enhanced energetic qualities	FOCUS

transformation of the soul and develop even deeper energetic qualities. Watch as they encourage the magic to unfold.

Feel the fire of inspiration with Spessartine Garnet in:
• Mirror gazing (see page 79)
• Golden channel meditation (see page 238)

Cultivate your magic with Galena, page 224
Engage in manifestation with Citrine, page 115

Mahogany Obsidian

The amount of time we spend distracted by life's responsibilities adds up quickly. Suddenly days go by where we haven't connected with our communities or immersed ourselves in the loving attention of nature. This isolation depletes our energy reserves. We become fatigued and listless, barely able to find the motivation to get up and out into the world.

We need connection with the Sun, the Earth, and our community. Without them our health deteriorates. Mahogany Obsidian encourages us to branch out for support by awakening memories of when we felt nurtured and alive with love.

Immerse yourself in nature to feel your energy reset. Step outside into the sun or sit under a tree. Is there something about your environment that feels out of balance? Where can you invite the guidance of Mahogany Obsidian to adjust your

Awakening, Shifting, Restoring	QUALITY
Root, Sacral	CHAKRA
Finding motivation, Reaching out for support, Adjusting perspective	FOCUS

perspective? It doesn't have to be a permanent shift, all it has to do is reinforce the fact that whenever we feel stagnant, movement can help.

Reset with Mahogany Obsidian in:
• Spending time outside
• Walking meditation (see page 30)

Embrace nature with Kambaba Jasper, page 49
Find the courage to shift with Green Opal, page 55

See images on pages 142-143

Peach Moonstone

QUALITY | Patient, Unfolding, Organic
CHAKRA | Sacral, Solar Plexus, Heart
FOCUS | Letting your life unfold in its own divine timing,
Appreciating the experience, Breaking from comparison

THE CRYSTALS

We've been so conditioned to value immediate results that it has trickled out into every aspect of life. We rush from place to place, we push for more efficient processes, we value increased growth and output, and if we do not see an indication of progress within seconds, our minds assume failure. This mindset has damaging consequences to society as a whole, but even more so on an individual level, where we are constantly comparing ourselves to others.

Every time we expect our growth to match those around us, we set ourselves up for disappointment. Each of us has a unique trajectory plotted out by circumstance and character - what works for one may not for another, or the pace at which it works may be different. Peach Moonstone reminds us that fruits ripen in their own time and so do we. We ensure the magic of divine timing by allowing the opportunity for that transformation to occur, organically.

Where are you rushing off to, and why the hurry? Stop what you're doing and stop assessing your success by comparing yourself to those around you. Lean into Peach Moonstone's sweetness and let yourself unfold naturally. There's no rush to arrive, but there is a whole lot of beauty to experience along the way.

Embrace more profound patience with Peach Moonstone in:
• Crystal yin yoga (see page 134)
• Sense writing (see page 212)

Feeling rushed? Head to Mookaite Jasper, page 57
Need a fresh start? See Cinnabar, page 136

Chrysanthemum Stone

"I am tuned into the communication of the universe, my heart is always listening."

Peach Moonstone

"I accept the divine unfolding of my life, there's no need to rush."

Mahogany Obsidian

"When my environment feels stagnant, I move."

Spessartine Garnet

"My actions create the reality of my dreams."

Golden Healer Quartz

"I surrender myself to
the divine, it will take
care of me."

Golden Healer Quartz

Supportive, Healing, Invigorating	**QUALITY**
Sacral, Crown	**CHAKRA**
Connecting to source, Reinvigorating enthusiasm, Opening up to energetic support	**FOCUS**

FIRE

Healing is a lifelong commitment. We get what we put into it. Many often forgo the experience as the process is intense and involved. It takes constant attention and requires us to surrender our will to the divine will. Yet, for those who make the effort, the reward is profound.

Golden Healer Quartz empowers us to surrender fully, providing a direct link to the universe's support and guidance. Its ability to keep us connected and engaged throughout our journey allows us to take great strides. Even recognizing the small accomplishments along the way makes a big difference. Golden Healer Quartz's warming embrace encourages us to shift our focus from being healed to enjoying the process of healing.

Notice where your own healing has stalled. What are the experiences or triggers that intimidate you, preventing you from continuing on? Open yourself up to Golden Healer Quartz's invigorating energy and allow it to inspire you to begin again. Let it keep you linked to source, enabling you to go deeper into your healing. The process may be endless but we are supported the whole way.

Jumpstart your healing with Golden Healer Quartz in:
• Golden channel meditation (see page 238)
• Breathwork (see page 156)

Attend to your heart with Pink Tourmaline, page 94
Connected to source? Go to Phenacite, page 245

Heliodor

QUALITY	Expansive, Guiding, Encouraging
CHAKRA	Sacral, Heart, Crown
FOCUS	Broadening perspective, Learning to take up space, Embracing change

The protective walls we build to keep ourselves safe limit our ability to see the bigger picture and our potential growth by keeping us contained. We operate under the illusion that what we see through our tiny window is all there is. There's no impetus to change. But the world is ever changing and we are part of that expansion whether we realize it or not.

When we restrict our growth, our vibration stutters and the light within us dims. It makes it increasingly difficult to manoeuvre. Heliodor guides us with elevated wisdom, lifting us out of the box and into the ether. The expansive view reminds us that there is a whole world outside and we should be a part of its transformation.

Open your eyes, open your heart. What are you able to see? Is your view restricted by your desire for security? Find a new vantage point. Be willing to embrace the challenge of different perspectives. Heliodor broadens our perception and in doing so inspires us to take up space and participate fully in life, reminding us that we create our own reality.

Embrace a new perspective with Heliodor in:
- Stargazing (see page 52)
- Breathwork (see page 156)

Heliodor

"The universe is an
expansive place, I keep
my mind open to
receive it all."

Break down the barriers with Galena, page 224
Take up space with Hematite, page 24

146

Jet
"I'm always supported.
I can always support."

Jet

Uplifting, Supportive, Connected	QUALITY
Root, Heart	CHAKRA
Embracing the power in your voice, Learning how to give and receive, Resilience	FOCUS

Hitting rock bottom hurts. It is scary and lonesome down there. Depression and sadness are long-term residents. Enthusiasm doesn't often visit here. Dropping down into this low place can be very upsetting. We see the long journey back up and wonder how, if ever, we can find our way out.

Whenever we find ourselves in the darkness of a deep well, we can rest assured that incredible transformation is imminent. Being at the bottom means we can only go up and Jet helps us bounce back by reconnecting us to our community. In the darkness we hear a friendly voice and make out the faint edges of an outstretched hand.

Acknowledge where you are at. If it is rock bottom, do you think you have to get yourself out of the depths alone? Jet reminds us that we are always connected and if we need support, the easiest way for it to find us is to use our voice. It also encourages us to listen carefully as maybe we are doing just fine, but we can be the helping hand someone else needs.

Bounce back with Jet in:
• Hand-holding meditation (see page 157)
• Chakra balancing (see page 156)

Afraid of the dark? See Snowflake Obsidian, page 27
Find connection with Cobaltoan Calcite, page 72

Bloodstone
"I nourish my body, mind, and soul with love."

Leopard Skin Jasper
"I am enough."

Bloodstone

	QUALITY
Rejuvenating, Releasing, Flowing	QUALITY
Root, Sacral	CHAKRA
Reinvigorating our circulation, Finding our flow, Nourishing the soul	FOCUS

The repetitive motions we engage in every day are tiny little traumas to our body, mind, and soul. They slowly build up, creating knots in the muscles and blocks in our energy. Because they form so gradually, we rarely realize the shift. It becomes our status quo. Our body forgets what it feels like for everything to be in alignment. Our energy forgets what it feels like to flow.

Our body, mind, and soul are hungry for nourishment, but the lack of circulation results in energetic fatigue and lethargy. Bloodstone restores our vitality, bringing us back to a place of grace and ease, where our energy flows freely.

Take a moment to get back in touch with your body, mind, and soul. Twist your body side to side, roll your neck around. Notice if you're holding a lot of emotion inside or if your mind feels foggy. These are indications that you need some rejuvenation. Call upon Bloodstone to inspire you to take care of yourself through rest, movement, or mindfulness. Find what feels good and watch your essence transform.

Feel the support of Bloodstone in:
• Massage and minerals (see page 134)
• Mineral nap (see page 182)

Cultivate a deeper release with Anhydrite, page 180
Get to the root of it with Fuchsite, page 24

Leopard Skin Jasper

	QUALITY
Accepting, Worthy, Compassionate	QUALITY
Solar Plexus, Heart	CHAKRA
Discovering our self-worth, Releasing the critical gaze, Bathing ourselves in loving acceptance	FOCUS

Society may have us believe that the expression our identity takes is not enough. It will offer us numerous options to improve the various imperfections, but even after all the work we'll still see our inadequacy. Is it even possible to feel sufficient as we are?

When we look at other animals, we commend them for their beauty and note how impeccably suited they are for their lives. The colourings and instincts help each animal live its purpose perfectly. Leopard Skin Jasper cultivates this deep acceptance of our own expression. It encourages us to recognize how our unique attributes enable us to live our destiny.

Look in the mirror. Are you seeing all the flaws that society says are unworthy? Try to look deeper. Breathe in, let your eyes relax their critical gaze, and notice three things about yourself that you appreciate. Channel Leopard Skin Jasper's considerate energy and embrace your whole vibration in compassionate acceptance.

Cultivate self-compassion with Leopard Skin Jasper in:
• Mirror gazing (see page 79)
• Divine light meditation (see page 157)

Still finding flaws? Let Pink Opal help you, page 109
Feel your beauty? Lean into it with Girasol, page 165

Sphalerite

QUALITY	Open, Appreciative, Dynamic
CHAKRA	All
FOCUS	Respecting other perspectives, De-conditioning, Letting information flow

We are conditioned to believe that there is only one right way. We prefer to have all the facts supporting our opinions to avoid contradiction. As we know, however, life is incredibly complex. The binary expression of our system forgets about the various shades that exist and intersect in between.

There is a full spectrum of expression existing out there. When we prioritize the binary, we miss out on the perspectives that guide us closer to harmony. Sphalerite urges us to include the wisdom beyond what any one single perspective can see. It asks us to prioritize equality. In doing so, we create a diverse choir that ensures each essence can live with dignity.

Pay attention to the way you embody conditioned expressions. Open up your mind and appreciate a perspective outside of your view. Let Sphalerite instil in you the idea that information is always coming and going. When we embrace this dynamic shift, our energy becomes more flexible and we lose the need to be right or wrong in favour of connecting from a place of openness.

Embody Sphalerite's inclusive energy in:
- Hand-holding meditation (see page 157)
- Gratitude practice (see page 78)

Expand your perception with Rutile, page 91
Challenged? See Pink Tourmaline, page 94

Stibnite

QUALITY	Calm, Harmonious, Aligned
CHAKRA	All
FOCUS	Connecting all parts of ourselves, Developing trust, Moving with intention

When we are confronted with a need to know, we rush out to uncover the answers. There's an immediate desire to have it all wrapped up and ready. Our rushing takes us out of harmony with our own rhythm. We disconnect from the aspects of ourselves that need time to process before the transition.

Stillness before action allows us to reflect and connect with the deeper parts of our energy. Stibnite tunes us into our vibration, enabling us to hear what our hearts are needing. The pause centres us and ensures we are moving in accordance with our highest good.

Trust that it will happen even if you move slowly - the urgency should not come at the expense of your energy. Let Stibnite teach you the value of intentional action, where you learn the art of reflection and how it can enable you to make wise decisions, even in the split-second moments. Embrace the stillness that allows you to fully engage with your own energy, ensuring every action is aligned with wherever you find yourself.

Explore deeper stillness and reflection with Stibnite in:
- Sense writing (see page 212)
- Crystal reading (see page 212)

Calm and centred? See Heulandite, page 236
Trust issues? Find support with Petalite, page 87

Stibnite
"In the stillness of my soul I discover aligned action."

Sphalerite
"I am open to many expressions of the universe."

Crocoite

"My passion guides me
through life."

Fluorapophyllite

"I recognize the responsibility
I hold within my community.
I nurture them with love."

Crocoite

Enthusiastic, Transforming, Inspiring	QUALITY
Sacral	CHAKRA
Connecting to our deepest passions, Harmonizing our energy, Discovering the possibilities	FOCUS

Passion is an extraordinary element for our personal transformation. When we tap into it we move towards our dreams with increased speed. Everything is possible, and we find endless amounts of motivation and determination to see things through. Under moments of stress and pressure, our passion can dwindle.

If the flicker of doubt finds a spot to creep in and upset this beautiful feeling you've been experiencing, Crocoite is the answer. It reinforces passion with love, vitality, and enthusiasm, which seal any energetic leaks we may have inside that drain our passion from us. It opens the mind so we become receptive to divine inspiration.

Explore your feelings right now. Where do you feel passion in your body, mind, or soul? Can you use it to inspire energetic transformation? If your reserves feel drained, let Crocoite suss out where the gaps are hiding. Lean into its restorative vibration to re-energize and align the heart. Embrace the sensation that relaxes all the tension in your energy so you can feel free.

Enhance your passion with Crocoite in:
• Sense writing (see page 212)
• Breathwork (see page 156)

Find your passion with Ruby, page 50
Energy leaking? Close gaps with Epidote, page 93

Fluorapophyllite

Inclusive, Connecting, Inspired	QUALITY
Heart, Crown	CHAKRA
Expanding community, Cultivating sincere relationships, Reciprocity	FOCUS

We are all interconnected. Our energy is always rippling out and, even without being conscious of it, we impact each other constantly. An inadvertent nudge could trigger angry words as much as a smile or kind gesture can create a spontaneous moment of loving connection.

There's a tendency to forget our connection to each other, seeing ourselves as individuals whose behaviour only affects ourselves. Fluorapophyllite helps transform our self-centred perspective into one of community responsibility.

Pay attention to your actions throughout the day to see how they stack up. Would they fall into the category of good for you or good for all? Fluorapophyllite emphasizes the integral role we hold in our communities and gives us the awareness to show up with sincerity. It inspires our heart to expand by reminding us that we are not alone. Anything one of us experiences affects the whole. It's up to us to ensure that our actions are uplifting each other with love.

Strengthen your relationships with Fluorapophyllite in:
• Hand-holding meditation (see page 157)
• Gratitude practice (see page 78)

Seeking connection? See Creedite, page 102
Explore community with Grape Agate, page 227

Chalcopyrite

QUALITY	Joyful, Radiant, Exciting
CHAKRA	Heart, Sacral
FOCUS	Finding purpose, Staying engaged and present in life, Remembering what brings you joy

Time passes in a blur and our days begin to follow a repetitive loop. The routine can make it difficult to find inspiration or follow our joy. Meaning and purpose feel like inaccessible commodities just out of reach. We keep going, lacking the zest to stay engaged, slowly numbing out.

Feeling alive is an amazing sensation and Chalcopyrite offers that to us as a humble gift. It helps us cultivate the excitement we need to break out of the numbing cycle and come back into our senses again. We learn how to use our inner radiance to enliven our path.

How is time moving for you? Do you still feel the excitement, or are you having difficulty feeling motivated to move with awareness? Anytime you find yourself lacking the oomph and interest to stay present and engaged, call upon Chalcopyrite to step in. It tickles the senses and awakens the spirit, bringing us back to life.

Enjoy the radiance of Chalcopyrite in:
• Mineral nap (see page 182)
• Chakra balancing (see page 156)

Delve deeper into intention with Pegmatite, page 96
Reconnect to time with Angelite, page 236

Zircon

QUALITY	Uplifting, Empowering, Sustaining
CHAKRA	Root, Crown
FOCUS	Remembering your abilities, Maintaining steady progress towards your goals, Finding motivation

The most difficult part of any journey is when we are almost there and our excitement collides with our anxiety. The destination is somewhat in view, but still too far away to fully see. The effort already expended has been immense and it can be difficult to maintain a steady pace. We must use the reserves of our energy wisely if we want to make it all the way.

We started on the journey for a reason, giving up now feels out of the question. Invite Zircon's encouraging vibration to lift you up and remind you what you are capable of. Its illuminating quality will make you believe in yourself again, and keep you moving steadily forwards towards your goal.

Maybe you've contemplated giving up or don't know how to keep going. These are natural thoughts to experience whenever we are challenging ourselves to the extreme. Zircon helps us remember why we began and what we have learned about ourselves in the process, cheering us on when the going gets tough. It keeps us motivated by reminding us of what awaits us at the finish line – satisfaction.

Keep pushing forward with Zircon in:
• Crystal yin yoga (see page 134)
• Breathwork (see page 156)

Remember your intention with Cuprite, page 65
Embrace your progress with Iolite, page 192

Chalcopyrite

"I live with joyful
radiance."

Zircon

"My intention keeps
me aligned even when
the path is hazy."

Transforming the soul

The convergence of breath and visualization results in an alchemical process that dynamically shifts our energetic vibration and reveals the magic and beauty that has always existed within us. These practices support the energetic alignment of our chakras – the major energy centres of the body – and our spiritual evolution.

Breathwork

Wherever we find ourselves emotionally, mentally, physically, spiritually, there is a style of breathing to nourish us. Below are a few different breathing techniques to accompany your crystal meditations.

- Lower belly breath – Breathe in through the nose, pulling the breath down into the low belly, letting it expand out. Slowly exhale out of the nose or mouth pulling in the abdomen to fully express the breath.
- Breath of fire – This active breathing technique energizes the body, mind, and soul. It employs a forced exhale that passively draws in the breath on the inhale. Sitting upright in a meditative pose, exhale the breath by forcefully pulling in the abdomen. The breath will immediately be drawn in. Continue for about three minutes. It is not recommended for those who are pregnant or have heart or spine conditions.
- Holotropic breathwork - this is a dynamic style of breathing that moves energy and helps release stuck emotional patterns. It is best done with a facilitator. The breath, which is inhaled and exhaled through the mouth, requires a steady pace. Lying down, take two deep breaths in and one full exhale out. Breathe in deep through the mouth, pulling the breath into the low belly; the second inhale fills the upper chest. Exhale fully. Continue actively breathing for about 15-20 minutes before letting your breath return to its regular rhythm. Emotions may come up, so give yourself permission to feel.

Chakra balancing

Restore flow whenever energy feels blocked in a particular part of the body.

- Lying down, place a correlating stone on each chakra and/or visualize their energy radiating in that area.

- Use each breath to call your energy into alignment chakra by chakra.
- Envision the energy moving up and down through your centre line, paying extra attention to breathe into those areas where you feel the flow restricted. Keep breathing until you feel the kinks release.

Divine light meditation
For those moments when you are feeling hesitancy within your energetic vibration.
- Create a circle of stones around you and, sitting up straight, envision source energy flowing through your crown, down and around your body like a waterfall, blessing every cell with vigour, radiance, and joy.
- Envision any fear or essence of uncertainty being diluted with love and transforming into divine inspiration.
- Keep breathing deeply until you feel every cell nourished.

Hand-holding meditation
This meditation uses the hands as extensions of the heart to foster a powerful connection through spiritual and energetic intimacy.
- Intuitively select a stone before pairing up.
- Sit across from your partner so the knees touch and each of you has one hand resting on opposite knees, palm side up.
- Place the stone you chose in your partner's hand and then rest your hand on top of theirs so the fingertips rest gently on the wrist.
- Close your eyes and take a few centring breaths together before silently gazing into each other's eyes. Do your best to sit in silence for at least 10 minutes, allowing yourself to be seen and offering your partner the same in return.
- Share why you chose the stone you did and what it represented to you, as a message from the mineral to your partner.

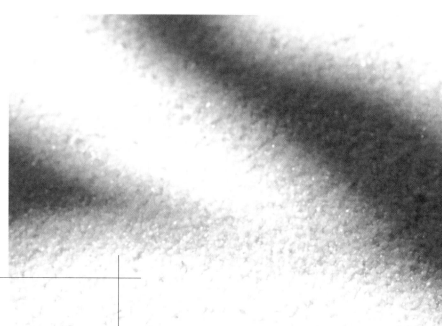

Ammolite

"Every experience
adds dimension to
my beauty."

Ammolite

In the moment of pain our focus is only on what we are currently feeling. The sensations can be intense, dredging up memories that cause us to lose sight of the fact that time heals all wounds. Without realizing, we perpetuate the discomfort and miss out on the beauty of our experiences.

These uncomfortable moments are what give us depth and character. We spend so much time complaining about the situation that we forget about our capacity to enact change. Ammolite, the opalized fossil of Ammonite, reminds us that transformation can occur under even the most unlikely of situations. All we need is time, patience, and perseverance.

Transcend your focus beyond the limitations of your ego, emotions, and senses. With this elevated perception, can you notice the depth your experiences impart on your soul? Following Ammolite's lead, let time create the layered dimension that transforms your most painful wounds, bringing the beauty and wisdom to the surface for all to see.

Undergo a deep energetic shift with Ammolite in:
- Reiki (see page 182)
- Divine light meditation (see page 157)

FIRE

Go deeper into your essence with Charoite, page 200
Change your perception with Labradorite, page 219

159

Enhydro Quartz

QUALITY | Protective, Ancient, Integrating
CHAKRA | Heart, Crown
FOCUS | Accessing the past, Revealing hidden feelings, Exploring the mysteries of life

Our ancestors gifted us the wisdom of their lived experiences. They flowed this wisdom through the generations, first as stories and then as intuition. This knowledge of the past is safely protected within us so that we can call upon it as we need it. All we must do to retrieve this wisdom is remember it's there to use.

Enhydro Quartz is the key to accessing our energetic gifts. The water held within it represents the potential that exists in all of us, the mystery of life that we nurture into existence. It supports the potential of our essence to be expressed through our interaction with the physical world. We can access the experiences that came before, opening us to endless possibility.

Envision the ancient droplets of wisdom passed down to you through your lineage. Had you forgotten they existed? As you explore each droplet, let Enhydro Quartz reveal the potential hidden within them. What new mystery can you unlock? What new possibility has been awakened?

Channel Enhydro Quartz energy in:
• Stargazing (see page 52)
• Water meditation (see page 182)

Explore mysteries with Iron Quartz, page 216
Connect to your ancestors with Spinel, page 133

Aquamarine

QUALITY | Expressive, Freeing, Honest
CHAKRA | Throat, Heart
FOCUS | Balancing emotions, Uncovering the emotional root of experiences, Creating space to feel

Expressing our feelings can be tricky. There's an emotional hierarchy where certain feelings are undesired or not appropriate for us to experience. We bury them deep inside, hiding them from the world. The truth is we're afraid of our big emotions. They reflect back to us the deeper longings of our soul, the imbalances that we are experiencing daily.

We keep our feelings hidden, assuming it will take the sensation away and make the world around us more comfortable. Is the world really comfortable, though, if everyone has feelings deep inside looking to be expressed yet there's no safety to do so? Every act of emotional suppression is deeply painful. We cannot help but feel. It is a part of our nature. Aquamarine helps us uncover the emotional root of our experiences and creates safe space for us to feel them.

Identify the emotions swirling within you. Are there any you avoid? Let Aquamarine liberate you and support connection with your undesired emotions. Can you appreciate their beauty and their complexity with more love and compassion? Remember, letting ourselves feel reinforces a sense of worthiness and invites greater emotional balance in return.

Create space to experience your emotions fully with Aquamarine in:
• Crystal yin yoga (see page 134)
• Breathwork (see page 156)

Soften your expression with Blue Lace Agate, page 168
Be bolder with your feelings with Aragonite, page 125

160

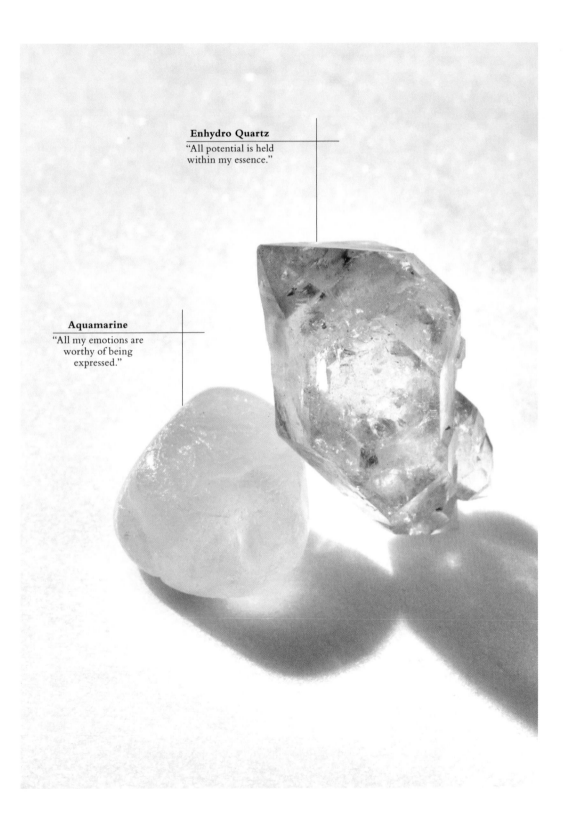

Enhydro Quartz
"All potential is held within my essence."

Aquamarine
"All my emotions are worthy of being expressed."

Larimar

QUALITY	Clarifying, Calming, Supportive
CHAKRA	Heart, Throat, Third Eye
FOCUS	Communicating feelings, Overcoming helplessness, Soothing the heart

Sometimes our emotions get out of hand. We may begin using them as a way to be noticed by others, or we may be using them to deflect from connection. Falling into a spiral of victimhood reflects a deeper hurt that resides within the heart. It is a pain created from our emotions not being seen or heard. We start identifying behaviour that gives us the attention that we crave. At the end of the day, all we want is to be loved.

Only something incredibly calming can help us move away from that painful sensation. Larimar is the clarifying force that soothes our aches and reminds us that things can change. It pulls away whatever it needs to reveal what's deep within the heart, purifying our emotional expression to guide us away from feelings of helplessness towards our emotional truth.

Reflect back on the last month, remembering the wave of feelings you experienced. Were there any that made consistent appearances? What emotions do you rely on to get attention from others? When our heart aches, or anytime there's a feeling within that wants to come out, Larimar is our friend. We learn the power of sincere emotional expression, allowing our true feelings to the surface.

Feel the flowing energy of Larimar in:
• Water meditation (see page 182)
• Ritual bath (see page 182)

Keep flowing with Wavellite, page 172
Develop your resilience with Desert Rose, page 29

Abalone

In a world built around possessions, where everything is about the physical, it can be difficult to cultivate a connection to source. There seems to be no room for it, but the world desperately needs it. Our spirit struggles to find its place in this material world.

An active spiritual mind creates an environment of peace around it. Our spiritual mind allows us to be open and receptive to the divine energy that guides us. Abalone stimulates the energy field, opening it up so we may connect to the divine. It ensures that we are compassionate and awake to the wonders and mysteries of the world as well as to the purpose we have within it.

Check in and see how your energetic vibration is doing. What's the status of your spiritual mind? How open are you to the universe's wisdom? With

Compassionate, Awakening, Strengthening	**QUALITY**
Sacral, Solar Plexus, Heart, Third Eye	**CHAKRA**
Opening intuitive connections, Creating peaceful environments, Activating the spiritual mind	**FOCUS**

Abalone's support, our mind is awakened and strengthened. We feel the inner connection of the universe and are ready to begin living with intention.

Awaken your spirit with Abalone in:
- Chakra balancing (see page 156)
- Divine light meditation (see page 157)

Find deeper peace with Celestite, page 209
Ready for universal wisdom? See Azurite, page 235

Blue Chalcedony

When we are centred within ourselves, grounded in our own energy, our intuitive awareness has an all-knowing clarity. The feeling of knowing without actually knowing, of feeling our intuition flowing is a wild ride that guides us to experience magical things. How do we nurture this part of ourselves more deeply?

As with anything, it is through practice – it's like a muscle to be used and stretched. Blue Chalcedony helps us train our intuition, providing the environment we need to deepen it. We feel calm, willing to explore our depths and get closer to the fears that have stood in our way. It helps us create clear boundaries around our own emotions and those we have picked up from others, so our intuition isn't affected.

Tap into your intuition. Are there messages from the universe waiting? Use Blue Chalcedony's

Insightful, Centring, Supportive	**QUALITY**
Third Eye, Throat, Crown	**CHAKRA**
Developing awareness, Strengthening intuition, Creating emotional boundaries	**FOCUS**

guidance to understand the whispers you may have misread. Let it bring you back into alignment with your inner truth so you can find that magical place of knowing.

Deepen awareness with Blue Chalcedony in:
- Crystal contemplation (see page 213)
- Aura meditation (see page 213)

Move back into the body with Green Calcite, page 43
Work on boundaries with Rhodocrosite, page 133

See images on page 164

Blue Chalcedony

"I open myself up to the
whispers of the
universe."

Abalone

"My heart and eyes
are open, I'm ready
to receive wisdom
from spirit."

Larimar

"I offer my emotions
space to be witnessed."

164

Girasol

Content, Reflective, Curious	**QUALITY**
Third Eye, Crown	**CHAKRA**
Learning to grow from a place of satisfaction, Seeing the truth in one's experience, Living in alignment	**FOCUS**

Girasol

"My curiosity
inspires my growth."

WATER

We compare ourselves to one another all the time. We see what another has, what others are doing, and pangs of jealousy arise within. We want what they have. The life they live appears so wonderful from our perspective. Our life pales in comparison. We don't see the beauty in who we are or what we do. Nothing is ever enough. We are never enough.

Living life focused on what others have takes you away from being able to appreciate what is around you. It prevents you from seeing your life as significant and worthy. Girasol helps us see ourselves more clearly, reflecting back to us in the mirror that who we are is exactly who we need to be in this moment. Everything about us is enough. We see the truth in our reflection and our experience. We are compelled to grow from a place of satisfaction, where the people around us are inspirations and reminders of what is possible, not our competition.

Take a look in the mirror. What do you see? Are you content with your reflection? The answer should always be yes. Girasol helps illuminate where we could find more contentment in our experience. It encourages us to grow from a place of curiosity and wonder, breaking us free from lack. The opportunities and potential are endless, but we must first start by recognizing the beauty in who we are and what we have.

Find the beauty within with Girasol in:
• Mirror gazing (see page 79)
• Reiki (see page 182)

For self-appreciation see Strawberry Quartz, page 83
Find beauty within with Amethyst Flower, page 215

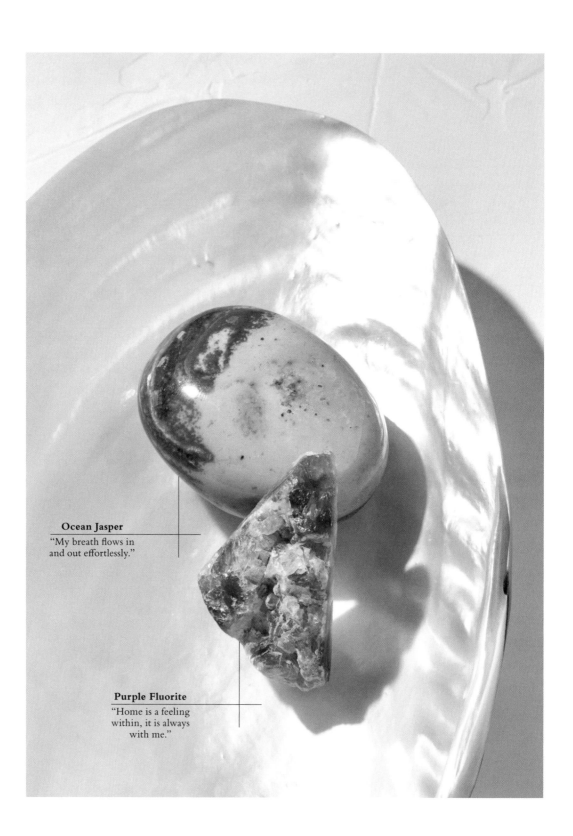

Ocean Jasper
"My breath flows in and out effortlessly."

Purple Fluorite
"Home is a feeling within, it is always with me."

Ocean Jasper

Life is endless chaos. So much is happening all the time that we often feel lost at sea - imbalanced, overwhelmed, ungrounded - the chaos rippling out, creating waves and affecting our surroundings. We also get knocked around by each other's energy and finding a sense of stability can be challenging.

The easiest way to feel calm is through the breath. A deep breath in and a deep breath out immediately slows down our vibration. But when we are floating, we need a little more help. Ocean Jasper is our guide, helping us navigate the stormy seas of life. We discover the rhythm of the water and the art of buoyancy. Our breath finds its fluid motion and we learn to move with the waves gracefully.

We never know when life's chaos will toss us out to sea. It can be scary to find ourselves adrift.

Soothing, Centring, Rhythmic	QUALITY
Sacral, Solar Plexus, Heart	CHAKRA
Uplifting energy, Calming the collective energy, Keeping the meditative breath flowing	FOCUS

Navigate the turbulence around you with Ocean Jasper's steady rhythm. Breathe slow and deep, letting your breath calm your spirit. Soon you'll find yourself ashore.

Keep energy flowing with Ocean Jasper in:
• Water meditation (see page 182)
• Ritual bath (see page 182)

Keep flowing with Larimar, page 162
Embrace chaos with Chrysanthemum Stone, page 140

Purple Fluorite

Think of the long trip home and the challenges we know we will face. Our longing to be held, to feel safe, motivates us to keep going, looking forward to the day when we will find ourselves back from where we came. But the home we left may not be the same as we remember. We wonder if we'll ever again feel that sense of security and clarity that home brings.

Whenever we are questioning or curious, or unsure and need to feel safe, Purple Fluorite finds and welcomes us with arms wide open. It holds us in its energy until the dust settles and we can clearly see the way. Nurturing us back into our body we learn to honour how we feel and respect our boundaries. It reveals the truth and dissolves illusions that may hinder our journey.

Reflect on the parts of your heart that have been looking for answers. What are you missing?

Welcoming, Clear, Cleansing	QUALITY
All	CHAKRA
Finding our way home, Honouring our boundaries, Discovering the answers	FOCUS

Let Purple Fluorite guide you back into yourself, teaching you to ground and find home within. Everything you seek is there, no matter where you may be.

Find what you need with Purple Fluorite in:
• Serene silence (see page 238)
• Reiki (see page 182)

Explore truth with Datolite, page 111
Find your foundation with Turquoise, page 46

Blue Lace Agate

QUALITY	Confident, Calm, Eloquent
CHAKRA	Throat, Solar Plexus
FOCUS	Expressing your feelings clearly, Honouring your boundaries, Responding from a place of inner serenity

Communication is a part of life, one of the key ways in which we connect with the world around us. When we have deep and complicated feelings to share, our words do not seem to come when we need them. Fear takes over and we withhold our deepest feelings, afraid of what will happen if they are expressed.

When we shy away from sharing our thoughts and feelings, we lose the opportunity to connect with vulnerability or to have our needs or desires heard. Like a gentle wave, Blue Lace Agate soothes the fear we hold around having our expression rejected or misunderstood. It helps us keep our cool and navigate the bumps of conversation with confidence.

Take a deep breath whenever you are struggling to express yourself. Remain calm and watch as Blue Lace Agate guides you towards the words that will allow your deepest feelings to be heard. Feel the sense of confidence emerge from the expressive eloquence it invokes. Know that whatever is inside eager to come out will find its way to the surface.

Uncover Blue Lace Agate's soothing power in:
• Stones on the body (see page 30)
• Crystal yin yoga (see page 134)

Communication blues? See Serandite, page 98
Cultivate confidence with Pyrite, page 126

Pearl

QUALITY	Embracing, Transforming, Mystical
CHAKRA	Sacral, Heart
FOCUS	Turning challenges into things of beauty, Protecting through welcoming, Finding solutions

Every day we are confronted with situations that irritate us. Little happenings that annoy, frustrate, or disrupt our flow. Thrown off course, it's easy for us to get caught up in our feelings about what we are going through. Very seldom do we think of what the experience can teach us or even how we can address it with love.

Our first response is a desire for the discomfort to leave. But, what happens if we welcome it? What happens if we try to work with the frustration? The act of acknowledging and reflecting has the potential to transform the thing that we resist, little by little. Pearl embodies the power in embracing that which has entered into one's experience uninvited. It shows what is possible when we respond to pain with love and compassion. The thing that irritates becomes an expression of beauty.

Inevitably something will make its way into your world and cause you distress. Soften your response. Slowly address it with loving awareness. Create your own pearl of wisdom that only arrives after time spent acknowledging your experience. Let your essence transform it into something beautiful. Like the irritation that makes its way into the oyster shell, slowly over time the discomfort becomes a testament to our resilience and magic.

Channel the embracing nature of Pearl in:
• Reiki (see page 182)
• Serene silence (see page 238)

Let it go with Angelite, page 236
Find peace with Pink Opal, page 109

Blue Lace Agate

"My words flow
through me with
clear confidence."

Pearl

"I welcome whatever life
brings and transform it
into beauty."

Sillimanite
"I appreciate the deeper purpose of life. Every piece of it is significant."

Sillimanite

QUALITY	Euphoric, Stimulating, Appreciative
CHAKRA	All
FOCUS	Expanding the perspective, Seeing everything as purposeful, Moving beyond the self

Everything has a purpose in the universe. Pieces are not weighted against each other, and each is playing a necessary and significant role. Yet, we tend to view those parts that are directly linked to ours as being more valuable. We see the relationship as indicative of significance, making harmonization difficult.

How will we ever make sense of the complexity of the universe if we limit our appreciation to only that which affects us? Sillimanite stimulates our wonder at the greater connections that keep everything moving, bridging the gaps in our awareness. We develop a sense of euphoria as we uncover the layers of existence, elevating the mundane into the divine.

Challenge yourself to go deeper. What are you closing off because you assume it has no relationship to your existence? Sillimanite encourages you to welcome in the energetic expression beyond the self. It shows us how even the smallest drops have expansive ripples.

Expand your awareness of life's interconnectedness with Sillimanite in:
- Stargazing (see page 52)
- Serene silence (see page 238)

Embrace euphoria with Orange Calcite, page 130
More harmony please! Flip to Hiddenite, page 72

Rainbow Moonstone

Perceptive, Hopeful, Intrepid | **QUALITY**
All | **CHAKRA**
Navigating life with openness, Taking chances, Transitions | **FOCUS**

WATER

Life is an endless set of doors for us to open. It takes courage to open them, let alone walk through them. How many times do we see a door and our hesitation over the uncertainty of what hides behind it prevents us from ever reaching for the handle? It feels safer to stay on the side of the familiar, no matter how unsatisfying.

Rainbow Moonstone gives us confidence to move through those moments of hesitation. It shows us that behind every door is another door. If what we find doesn't feel right, we can keep moving.

Have you lost your ability to embrace the possibilities of life? Or are you having trouble letting go of the past? Take a deep breath and reach for a new door. Enjoy Rainbow Moonstone's empowering energy that shifts your perception to one of hope and excitement. Lose your fear of what lies ahead and let go of attachments to the past, taking a chance to discover the wonderful mystery behind whichever door you open.

Explore the doors of possibility with Rainbow Moonstone in:
• Divine light meditation (see page 157)
• Walking meditation (see page 30)

Rainbow Moonstone

"I embrace each moment with openness. I do not hesitate to live life fully."

Take a chance with Rhodonite, page 93
Afraid to move forwards? See Sunstone, page 129

Blue Fluorite

QUALITY	Truthful, Calming, Purifying
CHAKRA	Throat, Third Eye, Crown
FOCUS	Addressing fear, Expressing yourself openly, Purifying the mind

There's a fear we hold of living honestly. We are afraid that the truth may hurt. We're afraid that the truth will force us to reject or be rejected. And so the feeling of connection between the people in our communities decreases. Anxiety builds, distorting our actions and perception. What is life if it is not lived with integrity?

Whenever fear becomes our obsession, Blue Fluorite cleanses our expression, purifying it with peace and love to heal the fragmentation in our soul. Energetically calm, we can be present and vulnerable. Our intuition deepens with its support, helping us to pick up on the nuance of our experiences so we can see them for what they are instead of the version our fear created.

Address your fear directly. Where has it been affecting your ability to connect and live in integrity? Has it impacted your capacity to communicate openly and honestly? Reclaim your power with Blue Fluorite's aid to smooth the aura, enhancing your ability to communicate from the heart. Remember that vulnerable expression facilitates growth and deepens our connections.

Clear fear from the aura with Blue Fluorite in:
• Aura meditation (see page 213)
• Water meditation (see page 182)

Use fear to inspire with Tangerine Quartz, page 129
Find deeper relaxation with River Rock, page 41

Wavellite

QUALITY	Flowing, Rejuvenating, Balancing
CHAKRA	Sacral, Heart
FOCUS	Exploring your emotional depths, Clearing the mind, Finding the neutral state

Emotions reflect the responses we have towards our world and experiences. Feelings become synonymous with our status quo. It becomes quite easy to get lost in our feelings when they take up so much of our mental space. The constant emotional stimuli can be exhausting and difficult to navigate.

Wherever we are getting caught up, Wavellite helps us find balance through the movement of our emotions. It rejuvenates our energy, getting us back in the flow of our natural, neutral state. We understand how to feel our emotions and absorb their wisdom without having them remain indefinitely, finding greater release and a sense of freedom.

Explore your feelings over the last week. What emotions did you have and are you holding onto them? Wavellite teaches us that we have definition outside of our emotions. We stop feeling the pressure and the overwhelm as we learn to accept that our feelings are just feelings passing through, we don't need to hold onto them.

Keep your emotions balanced and flowing with Wavellite in:
• Sense writing (see page 212)
• Crystal yin yoga (see page 134)

Struggling to let go? See Shattuckite, page 112
Clear the mind with Ametrine, page 235

Blue Fluorite

"I breathe in love and
my fear disappears."

Wavellite

"Emotions do not
define me, I allow
my feelings to flow
on through."

Chrysocolla

"I use my words to
uplift and empower
the conversation
with love."

Coral

"I filter my inspirations
through the heart to know
which I should follow."

Chrysocolla

Communication is one of the key ways in which we connect with each other, and is a significant aspect of building community. There's a slippery gravitation towards connecting through fear-based expression, which is used to create otherness. We become lost in criticizing, complaining, comparing, or using our expression to build ourselves up by knocking another down.

There is so much power not only in the words we use but in how we use them. When we communicate out of fear, Chrysocolla reminds us to realign our vibration to the heart. It empowers us to use our voice to speak with vulnerability and kindness, to ourselves and others, strengthening our sense of self-worth and our communities.

Have you fallen into the spiral of fear-based communication? Or maybe you've been around people who have and feel discomfort?

Empowered, Social, Guiding	QUALITY
Heart, Throat, Solar Plexus	CHAKRA
Heart-centred communication, Building community, Releasing fear	FOCUS

Chrysocolla reinforces the intention that if we speak with love, fear will not have a place in the conversation.

Prompt deeper connection through your communication with Chrysocolla in:
• Hand-holding meditation (see page 157)
• Love notes (see page 78)

Expand vocabulary with Herkimer Diamond, page 216
Keep moving beyond fear with Mesolite, page 210

Coral

Our lives embody the constant flow of energy, moving in response to the stimuli of the environment. Slowly building and expanding as the imagination allows. The more our creative flow is nurtured, the greater the dreams and the possibility of their manifestation.

It is up to us to keep exploring our inspirations and creating the opportunity for them to be realized. We can determine which inspirations feel in alignment – not every idea has to become something. Coral embodies this quality of discernment, demonstrating the importance of filtering everything through our aura for a quick evaluation. We learn to pass on the ideas not meant for us and to focus our energy on the ones that truly excite.

Jot down all the ideas swirling in your head. One by one, filter them through your aura for

Discerning, Imaginative, Symbiotic	QUALITY
Root, Heart, Third Eye	CHAKRA
Nurturing dreams into reality, Making decisions from an aligned energetic state	FOCUS

guidance on which feel in alignment. How many are left? Coral teaches us that we don't need to follow every inspiration, just the ones that truly resonate within.

Use Coral to keep imagination flowing in:
• Ritual bath (see page 182)
• Daily journalling

Need inspiration? Turn to Serpentine, page 136
Align your energy with Smoky Quartz, page 54

Rose Quartz

QUALITY	Comforting, Nurturing, Gentle
CHAKRA	Heart
FOCUS	Returning to love, Relaxing the critical gaze, Seeing ourselves with compassion

In a world where everything exists in constant comparison, we are forced to navigate feelings of insignificance and imperfection. Our hard, inflexible mind doesn't have the space to accept us as we are. The critical eye quickly emerges to evaluate our worth and we lose the ability to see ourselves clearly, preventing a deeper, more compassionate assessment.

There always seems to be something wrong that must be changed so we can be loved. Rose Quartz softens our perception, helping us to invite more gentleness into our expression. We notice where we have been too abrasive towards ourselves and others. We learn to receive and be nurtured by the energy of pure love.

Comfort the aching parts of your soul. Where have you restricted yourself from seeing who you are with eyes of love? Remember that love is an endless and unconditional vibration. Can you open your heart up and let yourself feel accepted? Rose Quartz goes beneath the surface feelings, deeper into the heart, keeping the love flowing in and out, nurturing us completely. Whenever our sight tightens up with fear, it helps us release the tension and return to love.

Find your way back to a loving vibration with Rose Quartz in:
- Love notes (see page 78)
- Reiki (see page 182)
- Heart flow (see page 31)

Shake judgment with Pink Mangano Calcite, page 85
Expand the heart with Morganite, page 228

Sapphire

QUALITY	Prophetic, Hopeful, Insightful
CHAKRA	Throat, Third Eye
FOCUS	Focused meditation, Calming the effects of external stimuli, Receiving and employing insight instantly

In order to receive guidance from the divine, we have to keep our energy aware and receptive. Insight is a magical gift from the energetic realm, received when we take time to pause and quiet the mind for reflection. The stillness lets the dust settle, offering us increased clarity around whatever is showing up in our lives.

We may think it necessary to be in total silence away from any outside stimuli, but the alignment of energy integrated with the world's chatter can actually encourage insight to the surface. Sapphire is the essence that helps us come back around, quieting the external noise just enough so that we can connect these forces for our illumination.

Take a pause and meditate. Where is your mind losing focus from outside interference? Can you harness the mental space for spiritual development? Cultivate the energy that enables insight to find its way through your aura. Let Sapphire bolster your mind with its focused vibration.

Sapphire supports a clear and open mind for meditation. Use in:
- Mineral nap (see page 182)
- Serene silence (see page 238)

Let the meditation flow with Ocean Jasper, page 167
Align your energy with Brookite, page 66

Rose Quartz

"Love is flowing
within and around
me endlessly."

Sapphire

"I cultivate stillness
to allow insight the
space to arrive."

Hemimorphite

"I am ready to
let go of the past
and embrace my
spiritual evolution."

Hemimorphite

Evolving, Joyful, Empathetic	QUALITY
Throat, Third Eye	CHAKRA
Deepening empathy, Developing emotional intelligence, Facilitating spiritual growth	FOCUS

WATER

Our sacral centre holds the wisdom of our lived experience, which allow us to develop empathy and a deeper emotional intelligence. This awareness empowers us to let go and embrace our spiritual evolution, integrating the wisdom so we may grow from it.

Taking the emotional memory locked within our bodies can be extraordinarily triggering, but it is these challenges that dynamically create the necessary force for our empathy to be developed. The changes in temperature or pressure that induce the piezoelectric quality in Hemimorphite show us the power we receive from undergoing such experiences. The energetic force field created in the process invigorates our energy and inspires a powerful enthusiasm that directly supports our spiritual ascension.

Notice where you have the greatest empathy. Recall the situations that enabled you to hold that emotional awareness and compassion. Can you apply the same process to your other experiences, expanding the breadth of your emotional intelligence? Under Hemimorphite's guidance, we can embrace the expansion of our empathy, increasing our ability to feel joy exponentially, as we share the message that we don't have to hold the heavy feelings alone.

Channel the invigorating energy of Hemimorphite to expand your empathy in:
• Hand-holding meditation (see page 157)
• Gratitude practice (see page 78)

Embrace your emotions with Aquamarine, page 160
Explore community with Jadeite, page 61

Blue Topaz

QUALITY | Truthful, Aligned, Attuned
CHAKRA | Throat, Heart, Crown
FOCUS | Channelling inner wisdom, Maintaining honesty, Regulating energetic intention

There is a difference between physical and energetic desire. The former keeps us locked in attachment where we need more to feel complete. The latter is a state of being that we can continuously cultivate. When we focus on the energy we are able to remain honest with ourselves and keep our intentions aligned.

Discerning the deeper expressions of what we desire can be challenging. We may easily find our vision swayed by the physical representation, forgetting the greater energies at play. Blue Topaz attunes us to our truth, helping us channel the inner wisdom that will guide us towards the opportunities that are aligned and supportive of our dreams.

Evaluate your desires. Are they stuck in the physical realm? Try moving beneath the surface to discover their energetic roots. What energies do these physical desires represent for you? Blue Topaz can guide you towards the true intentions of your desires, enabling you to expand the possibilities for their manifestation.

Ensure an energetic focus behind your desire with Blue Topaz in:
• Wishing ritual (see page 79)
• Crystal reading (see page 212)

Content? Find your way to Alexandrite, page 241
For manifestation energy see Citrine, page 115

Anhydrite

QUALITY | Tranquil, Releasing, Resilient
CHAKRA | Sacral, Throat, Third Eye
FOCUS | Navigating transitions, Transformation through loss, Embracing fluidity

One moment everything is going smoothly and the next, life has thrown you a surprise. The shock disorients you and the loss or dramatic shift takes away your breath, leaving you spinning in place. Maybe you feel like you cannot go on, or that you cannot fathom a world different from what you once knew.

Anytime we are navigating extreme transitions and lose the sense of tranquility that enables us to respond with a clear mind, Anhydrite comes to offer its support. At one time this mineral was Gypsum, and when it lost all water, it transformed. We see through Anhydrite's own experience of becoming that even when we lose something integral to our identity, our essence still remains.

Following the cycle further, we discover its ability to transform back into Gypsum if water returns. The lesson we learn here is one of grace, where we maintain a fluid expression that can adjust and survive regardless of the situation.

Reflect on your identity. What aspects of who you are feel fragile and dependent on anything other than yourself? Anhydrite reminds us that we can shift and change our expression as the circumstances require, but our essence will always remain. You will always be you.

Whenever you fear losing yourself, embrace a fluid identity with Anhydrite. It supports:
• Mirror gazing (see page 79)
• Water meditation (see page 182)

Let yourself flow with Ocean Jasper, page 167
Fuel energetic transformation with Tektite, page 246

Blue Topaz

"I see deep love wherever
there is truth."

Anhydrite

"I am, I am, I am and
I always will be."

Rejuvenating with stones

As energetic beings, we hold so much within and often need to decompress and recalibrate. The practices below nourish us by creating the time and space for our bodies to relax, our minds to calm, and our souls to feel love.

Mineral nap

The inherent grounding qualities of crystals make them natural restorative aids. Whenever you're feeling overwhelmed, overworked, or foggy, take 30 minutes out of your day to recharge with this refreshing practice. Lay down with a crystal on your heart, under your pillow, or held gently in your hands and let yourself doze.

Ritual bath

Create your own ritual bath by blending water-safe crystals, essential oils, plants, and salts of your choosing into hot bath water. Give them a few minutes to integrate together before immersing yourself and relaxing. Saying mantras or doing a simple breathing meditation deepens the experience. The options are endless. Try a cup of Epsom salts, a piece of Black Tourmaline, eight drops of rosemary oil, and a few sprigs of fresh basil paired with a silence meditation for an incredibly powerful bath.

Reiki

Like the breath, reiki is a universal life force within and around us that instils energy as an expression of love and allows us to feel the connections between all things. Placing hands on or around the body is one of the many ways to bring awareness of this vibration back into the body, mind, and soul.

Feel this energy now by simply closing the eyes and placing one hand on the heart. As you breathe, notice the sensations within you. Enhance this practice by incorporating crystals. Follow the guidelines for Stones on the body (page 30) and then place your hand on top of each stone for a few minutes before moving to other hand placements.

Water meditation

Energetically, water embodies a soothing, cleansing, and rejuvenating vibration. We can embrace these qualities whenever we take a bath or shower, are near a body of water, hydrate, or even find ourselves caught in the rain. Begin by settling your gaze on the water's serene energy, allowing the sensation of its movement to inspire peace and calm within your aura. Visualize the essence of water flowing in or around you, clearing away whatever needs to be let go. Emerge from the moment relaxed and refreshed. Incorporate a crystal into the practice to imbue it with an added dose of spiritual intention.

Clockwise from top: Pearl page 168, **Girasol** page 165, **Spirit Quartz** page 225, **Snakeskin Agate** page 122, **Coral** page 175, **Larimar** page 162, **Pink Opal** page 109, **Amethyst** page 207, **Coral** page 175, **Celestite** page 209, **Danburite** page 205, **Rose Quartz** (centre) page 176

Blue Tourmaline

QUALITY | Cleansing, Soothing, Fluid
CHAKRA | Heart, Third Eye, Sacral
FOCUS | Embracing your emotions, Aligning the energetic body, Discovering the root feelings

Tears are usually associated with being upset or grieving, when they actually mark the pinnacle of emotion. They cleanse, they soothe, they move energy within, bringing us in touch with the roots of our feelings. Yet here we are in a world where it is often taboo to cry, to let our emotions reach their height. This restriction keeps the depth of our feelings unknown, even to ourselves.

How do we reclaim our emotions? How do we let ourselves feel them so that we know them fully and can let them pass through? Blue Tourmaline is a powerful aide when we have disassociated from our emotions and need to find our way back to feeling deeply. Its energy is a gently rocking ocean, lulling us into a synchronistic sensation of body, mind, and soul. We uncover the truth that all emotions are beautiful and profound – there isn't one that is better or worse than another. Energetically aligned, we remember the power in expressing our emotions truthfully and vulnerably, appreciating each for what it reveals.

Close your eyes and breathe deeply. Can you feel tightness or heaviness stuck in your aura? Give yourself permission to cry, to release whatever has taken up space within, remembering that emotions, regardless of what they are, must remain fluid to prevent stagnation. Embrace the soothing vibration of Blue Tourmaline to let yourself find the tears that will free your energy.

Explore the depths of your feelings whenever your energy feels tense. Let Blue Tourmaline support:
• Chakra balancing (see page 156)
• Crystal yin yoga (see page 134)

Keep up the feeling with Basalt, page 124
Cultivate release with Tangerine Quartz, page 129

THE CRYSTALS

Pink Halite

Purifying, Tender, Releasing	**QUALITY**
Heart	**CHAKRA**
Reorienting your energy, Creating space to feel, Seeing the hidden beauty	**FOCUS**

Thoughts have a way of spiralling out of control, exponentially growing within the mind and slowly overtaking the awareness of the heart. In this confused state we become guarded and suspicious, unable to see the love and beauty that surround us.

It can feel very unsettling to be caught in this energetic whirlpool, limbs flailing but not helping move us from a place of fear and chaos into one of calm and safety. Pink Halite purifies the mind, shifting us out of the spiralling movement and back into a gentle flow that softens the guards we have used for protection. Released and reoriented, we can begin to feel again.

Has your mind taken charge of your feelings? If so, are you in a state of awareness where you feel out of control? Pink Halite returns us to a state of flow. We reconnect with our heart centre, which offers us clear direction and allows tenderness to enhance our strength.

Reorient the mind to feel fully and see the beauty with Pink Halite in:
• Serene silence (see page 238)
• Heart flow (see page 31)

Soothe the mind with Howlite, page 220
Take your flow to a new level with Blue Jade, page 75

Blue Kyanite

Compassionate, Communicative, Connective	**QUALITY**
Throat, Heart	**CHAKRA**
Strengthening relationships, Vulnerable expression, Understanding the dynamics of truth	**FOCUS**

We forget that communication is a reciprocal process – we must listen as much as we speak. When we focus on our part of the conversation, we miss what was shared and respond from a place of ego or fear. There becomes a focus on being right and proving ourselves that affects our ability to connect with each other lovingly.

If we truly desire strong relationships based on mutual understanding and respect, we must honour each other's expression. Blue Kyanite demonstrates the power of compassionate communication, helping us to find the words to share our truth and receive another's with openness and love.

Recall those conversations that led to challenging interactions. Were you thinking about what you would say next instead of listening? Were you focused on enforcing the validity of your truth above another's? Blue Kyanite shows how we can forge connection through vulnerability and compassion.

Strengthen your communication skills with Blue Kyanite. Let it support:
• Hand-holding meditation (see page 157)
• Love notes (see page 78)

Expand your heart with Heliodor, page 146
Discover your truth with Ajoite, page 83

See images on pages 186–187

Marble

"The possibilities are
limitless, I can choose
whichever feels aligned
and move ahead
with confidence."

Pink Halite

"Even in the most
unsettling of situations,
my heart guides me."

Marble

Inspiring, Transforming, Dreamy | **QUALITY**
Third Eye, Sacral, Solar Plexus | **CHAKRA**
Revealing hidden potential, Releasing fear around what could be, Ideas manifesting into reality | **FOCUS**

Blue Kyanite

"When we communicate from the heart, we can hear the truth clearly."

When we dream, the details and the process never need to be clear. Our minds are free to explore and experiment. The pressure arises when we go to translate the vision into reality. Suddenly the details don't make sense and the path forward is cloudy. Paralysed by the uncertainty in our vision, we never move forward to take the dream to the next level.

Anytime we find ourselves floating in thought, unable to make the first move, it's helpful to feel our way through the dream again. Marble encourages us to see beyond the surface. We are shown the limitless possibilities that could arise from any given situation, enabling us, much like the sculptors of the renaissance, to recognize the potential hidden within. The real beauty emerges when we bravely start chipping away to bring our visions to life.

What dreams and goals have you feared because the details weren't completely clear? Take a chance on what could be. Channel the bold vision of Marble into your life and begin to find inspiration and motivation in the raw material, letting the rest take shape later on.

Find your inspiration with Marble and manifest your dreams into reality in:
• Creativity grid (see page 106)
• Serene silence (see page 238)

Blue Tourmaline

"My emotions flow freely. I receive their wisdom and they move on."

WATER

Increase your boldness with Sulphur, page 130
Unsure of what to do next? See Chiastolite, page 62

Wishing Stone

QUALITY	Joyful, Abundant, Wondrous
CHAKRA	Heart
FOCUS	Moving from scarcity to abundance, Building patience for your dreams to materialize

There are moments when our hearts desire something so big and wonderful, it hurts. Our dreams are inundated with visions of what it would feel like when it arrives. The joy is real. Then we wake up and the manifestation of our desire seems so far away, we wonder if it will ever come. Our excitement begins to hone in on the absence and we shift into a scarcity mindset.

When we are focused on the lack we are experiencing, it is hard to recognize the true abundance of life. If we open our eyes wider, everywhere we look are endless opportunities and discoveries for us to enjoy. Wishing Stones act as a reminder of the magic that is ever present. Their striking white bands of quartz show how the energy of the universe is capable of creating such perfect anomalies of nature.

Find some time to explore the outdoors. Let each breath of fresh air reframe your thoughts and help you see all the plentiful manifestations of the universe. Channel that energy into your Wishing Stone to set the intention, and keep your heart open for your desire to materialize.

Embrace the wonder of Wishing Stones in:
• Wishing ritual (see page 79)
• Gratitude practice (see page 78)

Wishing Stone
"I make my wish and release it unto the universe for manifestation."

Need inspiration? Flip to Orange Selenite, page 33
Feeling envious? Turn to Emerald, page 65

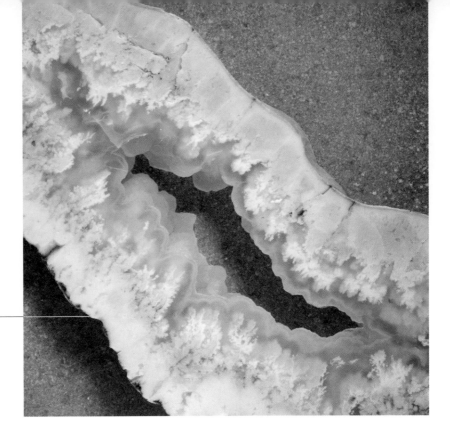

White Agate
"I take a deep breath
and every cell of my
being feels peace."

White Agate

Soothing, Releasing, Trusting	QUALITY
Root, Sacral, Heart, Crown	CHAKRA
Clearing your worry and anger, Moving on from trauma, Harmonizing your energy	FOCUS

Worry and anger are two of the most common feelings to plague our minds. If it isn't one, it's the other. We spiral into disastrous thought loops and anticipate trauma. We are ready to retaliate to protect ourselves, yet nothing has even happened. Locked into this fearful way of existing, our nervous system is always on guard.

White Agate is a harmonizer, balancing and grounding our physical and energetic bodies. Like a lullaby to the soul, the wispiness of its energy soothes the anxiety and anger so that we can feel completely restored. All aspects of our essence are held gently within its vibration. Our energy begins to trust again and in the process releases the narratives of trauma that have held us in fear for so long.

Have you been on edge lately, always looking over your shoulder or expecting the worst?

Maybe you feel ready for a change in energy and perspective. White Agate creates a serene environment - relax into it and let go of those stories that have kept you fearing the future.

Soothe your soul with White Agate in:
• Reiki (see page 182)
• Stones on the body (see page 30)

Channel anger into creativity with Cinnabar, page 136
Challenging feelings? See Leopard Skin Jasper, page 149

189

Copper
"My soul is filled with
purpose and life, I feel
vibrant and alive."

Tanzanite
"I open myself up to
the divine plan and
surrender myself
to the universe."

Copper

There we are, but we don't feel or look alive. Our enthusiasm is absent and the mind is drifting into numbness. There's no connectivity between our mind, body, and soul. We simply move listlessly around like the spirit within has been turned off and we cannot find the switch to turn it back on.

Sometimes we just need the spark to get us moving again – a dash of excitement or the unexpected to remind us of where we are and to inspire our energy with purpose. Copper is the perfect jolt to awaken us into action, stimulating our internal energetic circuitry. It gives us the oomph to begin, the motivation to continue, and the ability to dynamically change direction if what we are doing doesn't feel right anymore. It reminds us that we are brilliantly alive!

If you find yourself moving without purpose or presence, or you cannot muster the energy to

Energizing, Alive, Connective	QUALITY
Root, Sacral, Solar Plexus, Heart	CHAKRA
Stimulating our energy, Rekindling enthusiasm, Remembering the sensation of being alive	FOCUS

care or do, call upon Copper to stimulate your energy. Feel its current flow through your body, reminding you of what it means to feel alive.

Energize your soul and rekindle your enthusiasm for life with Copper in:
- Breathwork (see page 156)
- Divine light meditation (see page 157)

Feeling electricity? See Spessartine Garnet, page 141

Explore your numbness with Fire Opal, page 116

Tanzanite

We expend a lot of energy forcing our way through life, developing habits that hold us back. The repetition strains our bodies and minds, leaving little room for reflective growth. We lose touch with our intuition, creating further discord between our physical and spiritual essence.

The arrival into this moment where everything we try no longer works can be disheartening. Tanzanite prompts a deeper reflection into our intention and inquires where we have fallen out of alignment with our values. It helps us dissolve the habitual patterns that no longer support us, so we can move on from our habits with grace and ease.

Have you come up against a wall with no way around or through? Are you still trying what you've always tried? If so, it's time for some innovation. Tanzanite encourages us to surrender our will to the universe, while we focus on trusting

Transforming, Reflective, Expansive	QUALITY
Sacral, Third Eye, Crown	CHAKRA
Surrendering to the universe, Uncovering your values, Creating space for innovation	FOCUS

and showing up with openness. The more we allow our energetic transformation, the greater the space for the divine plan to get underway.

Open up to the universe's guidance with Tanzanite in:
- Divine light meditation (see page 157)
- Golden channel meditation (see page 238)

Develop greater trust with Soapstone, page 110

Become clearer on your values with Onyx, page 45

Blue Calcite

QUALITY	Nurturing, Balancing, Restful
CHAKRA	Root, Sacral, Heart, Throat
FOCUS	Understanding the needs of our energy, Reframing urgency, Taking time for oneself

There's always one more thing to do. An email to send or project to finish. We push ourselves to the limit. We wake up and do it again the next day, never allowing a moment for rest. How are we supposed to feel centred and balanced if we are always going, always doing, never consciously taking care of ourselves in return?

When we avoid listening to the gentle requests of our energy, Blue Calcite intervenes. It slows us down to better understand the effects of constant action and evaluates whether or not there's true urgency in what we are doing. The answers help us restore balance to our mind, body, and soul.

The body can handle quite a bit of wear and tear and stress, before it gives in. Why wait for that moment to nurture yourself? Blue Calcite translates your body's needs, guiding you to the type of care that would most rejuvenate. Caring for yourself is a radical act of love and you deserve it.

Listen to your body's expression of need and learn the best ways to nurture it with Blue Calcite in:
• Ritual bath (see page 182)
• Mineral nap (see page 182)

Lean into self-care with Amethyst, page 207
Struggling to slow down? See Sugilite, page 196

Iolite

QUALITY	Hopeful, Responsible, Buoyant
CHAKRA	Root, Heart, Crown
FOCUS	Inner-self awareness, Cultivating stillness, Actively participating in life

Where there is hope, anything is possible. Hope is a powerful energy that maintains buoyancy despite hardship. It has the capacity to galvanize people and ideas, even under the most unfavourable circumstances. We become bold champions and believers with just the smallest inkling of hope present, giving life to what may have been lost causes. Yet, hope can be hard to come by, and even harder to keep if we forget how to cultivate it.

Iolite is the seed of hope in crystal form. It teaches us the responsibility that goes hand-in-hand with hope, reminding us that we must be active participants in order for it to keep us uplifted. Guiding us to a place of stillness where we can become aware of our innermost self, Iolite helps us accept responsibility and acknowledge the truth, so that our ability to remain hopeful has lasting power.

Whenever hope is waning or you feel the urge to give up, call in Iolite to help you find your way back to a hopeful disposition. Channel its vibration into any area of life that could use hope's buoyancy, and allow its enthusiastic support to help you make it through the difficult times. Iolite's peaceful energy will strengthen your resolve and inspire conscious action.

Find stillness with Iolite in:
• Breathwork (see page 156)
• Serene silence (see page 238)

Gloomy perspective? See Black Tourmaline, page 63
Be an inspiration to others with Benitoite, page 200

Blue Calcite

"I listen to my body
and nurture it
with love."

Iolite

"Hope is the light in my
heart. It keeps me going
even when life is
challenging."

Black Moonstone

"The depths of my
soul have endless
wisdom."

Smithsonite

"With each breath,
my energy aligns
to the heart."

Smithsonite

Balancing, Loving, Transforming	QUALITY
All	CHAKRA
Centring the energy, Healing imbalances, Bringing us back in touch with our authentic self	FOCUS

The chakras of the body operate best when fully aligned. Out of balance they can begin to stagnate and disrupt our energetic flow. Even if it is only one that is out of line, the whole is affected. We feel this manifest as physical illness, mental confusion, emotional volatility, and spiritual disconnection.

Bringing our energy back in line requires us to explore the deeper roots of where we are out of balance. Smithsonite guides this exploration by uncovering the areas and healing them with loving kindness. As it slowly realigns our chakras, we feel calm and empowered, capable of handling the challenges and traumas of life, in the past, present, and future.

Can you sense an imbalance in your energy? Take this opportunity to embrace the supportive vibration of Smithsonite and realign your chakras.

Witness the profound transformation that occurs when everything is centred again and you are radiating your pure authentic self.

Cultivate your most radiant expression with Smithsonite in:
- Chakra balancing (see page 156)
- Divine light meditation (see page 157)

Increase your glow with Golden Topaz, page 51
Feel reverberations of the past? See Turquoise, page 46

Black Moonstone

Adventurous, Sacred, Accepting	QUALITY
Root, Sacral, Heart, Crown	CHAKRA
Healing the shadow, Rebirthing anew, Exploring the soul	FOCUS

Deep down in the well of our consciousness is where the shameful experiences or feelings of our present go to hide. We may avoid exploring this shadowy part of ourselves for fear of what we may find, but whatever is down here will always find a way out.

How do we gracefully express the shadow and turn it into a source of our empowerment? By becoming comfortable with our full, imperfect selves. Black Moonstone helps us fully appreciate everything that made us who we are. It offers us a chance to be rebirthed, bringing all our guilt and shame to the surface at the same time. We release their hold over us and can embrace ourselves with love, turning traumas into sacred wounds.

Explore the depths of your soul. What elements of guilt and shame are hiding down there? Welcome it all to the surface as Black

Moonstone does, and watch it transform your spirit into the powerful essence that is, and always has been, you.

Facilitate a spiritual rebirthing with Black Moonstone in:
- Ritual bath (see page 182)
- Breathwork (see page 156)

Find some courage with Red Jasper, page 42
For more soul exploration see Brookite, page 66

Shungite

QUALITY	Open, Honest, Purifying
CHAKRA	All
FOCUS	Transforming through vulnerability, Creating safe space for each other to show up authentically, Inspiring others

Vulnerability can seem like such a scary thing. It asks us to be honest, authentic, and brave in all situations and towards everyone. But the desire for love and acceptance complicates matters, creating the perfect storm instigating us to close off towards each other and project a version of ourselves that feels more palatable. This projection creates distance between ourselves and our communities.

In order to transform our desire for love and acceptance we must take time to balance and purify ourselves. Shungite guides this process wherein we reclaim our centre and call back the energetic projection. We create the space for ourselves to be seen authentically.

Inspire the world around you to be more vulnerable through your own willingness to also be vulnerable. Lean into Shungite's purifying vibration to keep compassion flowing, so that each member feels safe to show up and be seen without needing to hide parts of themselves. Watch the shifts that occur in your community when people are able to live in dignity.

Let your true self shine with Shungite in:
• Hand-holding meditation (see page 157)
• Mirror gazing (see page 79)

Struggle to be open? See Strawberry Quartz, page 83
Ready to be vulnerable? See Cuprite, page 65

Sugilite

QUALITY	Patient, Calming, Nurturing
CHAKRA	Root, Solar Plexus, Third Eye
FOCUS	Taking the time we need, Appreciating the process, Allowing the transformation to unfold as it's ready

The spiritual seeds we plant today take time to become the transformational harvest of tomorrow. We may feel eager to jump ahead, whether out of excitement or impatience, but it doesn't change the fact that the seeds need time to grow. There's no way to rush the process and no reason to either. Taking our expectation and ego out of the way creates a supportive environment for spiritual growth.

Patience and nurturing calm the energetic chatter that keeps us moving too quickly. Sugilite helps us develop these qualities to support our soul's evolution. We take pleasure in the process of letting the spiritual seeds develop and discover that there's much we learn along the way too.

Where are you rushing ahead in life? Can you take it a bit slower, enjoying each moment for what it offers? It's not always the end point that matters, it's often everything that happens in between. Listen to Sugilite's guidance and practise patience, remembering that we miss a lot of wisdom in the rush. Our growth is more exponential if we give it time, and we will relish the fruits more when they are ripe and ready.

Enjoy the unfolding of your spiritual growth with Sugilite in:
• Crystal yin yoga (see page 134)
• Gardening with stones (see page 52)

Move a little slower with Rainbow Fluorite, page 231
Nurture yourself more with Fuchsite, page 24

Shungite

"My heart is open and welcoming, I feel safe in my community."

Sugilite

"I savour the moments in between, watching the growth happen in real time."

Blue Apatite

"We accomplish
more together
than we do alone."

Blue Apatite

Empowering, Connective, Innovating	**QUALITY**
Root, Heart, Throat, Third Eye	**CHAKRA**
Navigating the twists and turns of life, Community building, Creating space for inspiration	**FOCUS**

Life comes at us fast, flying through as a gust of wind. Sometimes it's a welcome breeze after a long summer, at other times it's a windstorm that knocks us over. It all depends on the direction we're facing and whether or not we are bracing for its blow alone or with others.

Whatever the situation, Blue Apatite reminds us of the importance of coming together to navigate these experiences. Our energy is increased because we don't have to work so hard to move forward, allowing more time to enjoy all the sweetness that life has to offer. The empowering vibration cultivates creative innovation that comes from having the space for our intellect and creativity to emerge.

How are you facing life's surprises? Are you facing the gust headfirst, trying to move forward alone? Or are you coming together with your community, protecting, supporting, and empowering each other? Blue Apatite enhances our ability to work together, taking the pressure and weight off any one individual. We all emerge lighter and with more room to receive and act on our inspirations.

Channel the power in group work with Blue Apatite in:
- Breathwork (see page 156)
- Hand-holding meditation (see page 157)

WATER

Reconnect with community with Dravite, page 246
Embrace creative ideas with Ametrine, page 235

Charoite

QUALITY	Cleansing, Uplifting, Radiant
CHAKRA	All
FOCUS	Clearing the energetic body of external vibrations, Opening the heart for deeper connection

The energetic body is sensitive to the various stimuli of the environment. When we encounter a joyful or curious energy it can be refreshing. If the energy is frustrated or impatient, it can create tension. Regardless of the energy, though, we can become overwhelmed with vibrations that are not ours. This can begin to diminish our natural radiance and weigh us down.

The aura is the luminous body that surrounds your physical form. It extends far and wide, and is constantly coming into contact with the world around you. After a long day, you may feel the effects of so many energies crossing into your own. Charoite's vibration lifts the sluggishness that develops from carrying around the weight of other energies, transmuting them for a cleansing effect on the aura, restoring it to its natural glow.

Charoite reveals where the aura is too permeable to external interference and helps reinforce those spots so we can move and interact more comfortably. When our aura is bright and supported, we are able to interact with an open heart and mind, deepening our connections.

Receive an energetic reset with Charoite in:
- Aura meditation (see page 213)
- Massage and minerals (see page 134)

Work on boundaries with Rhodochrosite, page 133
Channel your radiance with Chalcopyrite, page 154

Benitoite

QUALITY	Curious, Connective, Considerate
CHAKRA	Crown, Third Eye, Throat, Heart
FOCUS	Finding pathways to understanding, Creating safe spaces to express, Learning how to reserve judgment

It takes a considerable amount of courage to share ourselves with others. Even more so when our beliefs or values are different. We are conditioned to keep those who hold opposing views at arm's length, silently passing judgment. This behaviour creates hostile environments that lead to more misunderstandings and harm.

While it's important to feel free to stand up for and voice one's beliefs, Benitoite reminds us how to do so with kindness and compassion. Our goal is not to prove our point, but create a safe space for each of us to express ourselves freely. It shows us how to approach the conversation from a place of curiosity that can help each party understand the deeper roots of each other's views.

Practise connecting with curiosity leading the way. How does that shift your relationship to those whose views are different from your own? Lean into Benitoite for guidance whenever you are feeling quick to judge or jump to conclusions. It doesn't mean you have to agree, the hope is it helps you discover a thread of common humanity.

Embrace Benitoite's wise energy whenever conversations feel tense in:
- Hand-holding meditation (see page 157)
- Compassion grid (see page 106)

For the art of communication see Creedite, page 102
Cultivate courage with Heliodor, page 146

Charoite

"My aura is radiant,
I nurture it with love."

Benitoite

"My curiosity keeps
my heart open to the
world around me."

Chlorite Quartz

"My heart is open and
filled with compassion."

K2 Stone

"My heart and mind are
open, I have arrived."

Chlorite Quartz

The more compassion we can offer one another, the better. It doesn't help us to be impatient or critical. We are all doing the best we can with the tools we have. Adding to each other's trauma exacerbates an already challenging situation.

It is in our compassion that we enable love to bloom, creating the supportive environments that nourish us. We must build a world where we look to create less harm for one another. Chlorite Quartz teaches us how through the essence of oneness, wherein what we do to others is done unto ourselves. When we recognize our connection to each other, and to the earth, we are more compelled to let our compassion come through.

Take a moment of introspective reflection and note where you could exercise more compassion. Sometimes the very act of seeing how often our

Expansive, Connective, Softening	QUALITY
Heart, Third Eye, Crown	CHAKRA
Discovering oneness, Opening the heart, Building a better world	FOCUS

impatience emerges is enough to help us shift our behaviour. Chlorite Quartz will purify your energy, offering a fresh perspective so you can become a more compassionate being.

Open your heart with Chlorite Quartz in:
- Hand-holding meditation (see page 157)
- Compassion grid (see page 106)

Soften your energy with Desert Jasper, page 36
Need more patience? Turn to Petalite, page 87

K2 Stone

Much of our experience is from the ground looking up to the sky. We feel the support of the earth and are comfortable here. There are some who feel compelled to explore greater heights. They go deep into the spiritual practices that will take them to the place where the earth meets the ether.

This juncture offers a feeling of grounded elevation, opening the mind and expanding the awareness of the soul. The effort it takes to make it there is extreme, and K2 Stone embodies that effort perfectly. It guides our spiritual expansion, giving us the strength and resolve to keep going.

Where are you on your spiritual journey? Are you feeling ready to embrace a new vantage point? Balancing our earthly expression with our spiritual ascension, K2 Stone takes us on an epic journey of transformation. It motivates us by

Monumental, Transcendent, Purposeful	QUALITY
Root, Crown	CHAKRA
Connecting the ground with the ether, Accessing divine inspiration, Spiritual growth	FOCUS

showing what lies on the other side of all the effort – the warmth of the sun on our faces looking out across the earth into the expressions of ether.

Soak in the view and enhance your spiritual growth with K2 Stone in:
- Serene silence (see page 238)
- Breathwork (see page 156)

Prepare for the ascent with Ammolite, page 159
Need a pep talk? See Watermelon Tourmaline, page 74

203

Lapis Lazuli
"I embrace the
mysteries of life
with openness."

Lapis Lazuli

QUALITY	Objective, Aware, Mysterious
CHAKRA	Third Eye, Crown
FOCUS	Truthful communication, Inner visioning, Self-examination

In the beginning, the world was a dark and formless field of energy, ebbing and flowing until the movement brought it into shape. This was a time before time even existed – raw, mysterious, and peaceful – where the answers to our existential queries live.

When we slip into this dimension, whether through a dream or deep meditation, Lapis Lazuli is there, waiting to guide us through the uncertain terrain. Facilitating a deep exploration into the past, it ushers us into an experience of total awareness, where we see the interconnectedness and evolutionary energy of the universe.

The journey here is not for the faint of heart, but for those courageous enough to explore themselves. Lapis Lazuli is a strict but supportive teacher, whose Lazurite blue tones will soothe the spirit, while the gold and white flecks of Pyrite and Calcite inspire and illuminate truthful self-examination. If we heed its advice, our physical, emotional, mental, and spiritual bodies will harmonize, leading us to understand the secrets of the universe.

Learn the lessons of time and space with Lapis Lazuli in:
• Stargazing (see page 52)
• Serene silence (see page 238)

Not ready for tough love? Try Spinel, page 133
Looking for adventure? See Magnetite, page 55

Danburite

Serene, Creative, Fortifying | **QUALITY**
Heart, Crown | **CHAKRA**
Support through grief, Relief of emotional pain, | **FOCUS**
Accepting oneself and others

Grief is a natural part of life and, as emotional beings, one we will inevitably encounter. The different forms of loss that arrive can challenge our ability to live fully and joyfully. We may become lost in our suffering, struggling to find our way through the discomfort.

Lifting us up for a breath of fresh air, Danburite carries us through the difficult times. It offers relief to our weary hearts and fortifies our energy, so that eventually we will be able to move forwards on our own. Once strengthened, we can channel our feelings into creative expression to honour our experiences and offer solace to others going through similar challenges.

We have all experienced emotional heaviness that has us question our ability to keep going. We may even feel like our world has ended. Danburite reminds us that we don't have to carry ourselves through it alone. The universe is here to love us and restore our faith that things will be OK, even though they may not seem that way right now.

Allow your grief and pain to be transformed under Danburite's sweet energy in:

- Heart flow (see page 31)
- Reiki (see page 182)

ETHER

Danburite

"Love lifts my heart
bringing me back
to serenity."

Transform emotions with Blue Tourmaline, page 184
Strengthen your support with Black Kyanite, page 27

205

Clear Apophyllite

"When I listen to my
inner truth, I know
how to move towards
my dreams."

Amethyst

"I allow myself the
opportunity to enjoy
the pleasures of life
guilt free."

Clear Apophyllite

Open, Aligned, Confident	QUALITY
Crown	CHAKRA
Remembering your intention, Taking action from a place of knowing, Listening to your inner wisdom	FOCUS

Sometimes in life it feels like we take two steps forward and four steps back. The dance of inspiration, action, and reflection is mixed with the stepped-on-toes of confusion and forgotten intention. We move forward without checking in to ensure that everything is still aligned.

Our high hopes and dreams are stumbling along because our focus is off track. We've lost sight of all the guidance within that opens up the path. Clear Apophyllite raises the sound of our inner voice, reminding us of who we are, what we need, and how to realign our energy. Under its vibration we slow down to let things settle, receiving the clarity we need to take action with confidence.

Connect to all that is within while cultivating a moment of serenity. Watch as your inner light and truth ignite in the stillness. Clear Apophyllite will help you hear your inner wisdom loud and clear, transforming your movements into a supportive and elegant stride that moves towards your dreams.

Embrace your inner wisdom with Clear Apophyllite whenever you find yourself backpedalling without reason. Try in:
- Mineral nap (see page 182)
- Crystal reading (see page 212)

Inspired? Step over to Dendritic Agate, page 22.
Shake off the chaos with Hypersthene, page 58

Amethyst

Conscious, Thoughtful, Soothing	QUALITY
Sacral, Crown	CHAKRA
Overcoming addictive tendencies, Balancing the physical and energetic bodies, Rediscovering pleasure	FOCUS

Finding balance between our responsibilities and rest is a constant learning process. We tend to feel the weight of our obligations in such a way that when we do have time to enjoy ourselves, we feel guilty. Bouncing back and forth between these extremes is unsettling, and begins to create unhealthy coping mechanisms.

Under Amethyst's gaze, we cultivate a sense of stability by living with awareness and intention. We learn to balance responsibility with pleasure, knowing there's a time and place for it all.

Addiction shows up in many ways, most notably when we make choices that go against our intentions. If we are constantly undermining all of our desires, it may be time to take a deeper look within and uncover the fear-based beliefs that are defining our actions. Amethyst reminds us that pleasure and joy are just as important as any responsibility. When we maintain conscious awareness and set clear intentions, the fear no longer disrupts and we begin to live a more balanced existence.

Let Amethyst inspire a reframing of your life in:
- Ritual bath (see page 182)
- Crystal contemplation (see page 213)

Embrace life's pleasures with Ruby, page 50
Set boundaries with Blue Chalcedony, page 163

Diamond

QUALITY	Strength, Brilliance, Perspective
CHAKRA	Root, Crown
FOCUS	Transforming under pressure, Remembering the lessons of the past, Observing without judgment

When life's pressures arise, we are quick to feel overwhelmed and disappointed. There's a desire for our experiences to always be pleasant and easy. The perfection we seek, however, is an illusion and inhibits our ability to transform.

Opting for perfection naturally leads to us evaluating our environment by making snap judgments. We lose objectivity when we overlook the deeper essences that exist. Take carbon, for instance, a plentiful element that at first glance would not seem so spectacular. Yet under immense pressure and heat, it transforms into Diamond, one of the strongest and most brilliant materials on earth. We can learn a lot from this transition, seeing each experience as an opportunity where what we once were becomes something so much more.

Observe the experiences of your life. Have you avoided the pressures, assuming they had nothing to offer you? Next time, surrender to them the way carbon does and relish in the strength and brilliance of your Diamond self that emerges.

Shift your perspective towards the challenges of your life with Diamond in:
• Breathwork (see page 156)
• Divine light meditation (see page 157)

Diamond

"Life's pressures transform me into my most radiant self."

Continue transforming with Pearl, page 168
Let your light shine with Golden Apatite, page 38

208

Celestite
"No matter where I go,
I'm exactly where
I should be."

Celestite

Throughout our life, we come to various points where the path splits and we must choose a direction. With little information beyond what we can immediately see, these decisions disrupt our energetic harmony. The fear of choosing incorrectly can keep us stuck in place.

These crossroads may feel intimidating, forcing us to overthink, but really what they offer is an opportunity to cultivate inner peace. Celestite facilitates this vibration by reconnecting us to the divine energy that alleviates the worry and fear. Feeling soothed, we can focus on which path feels the most aligned with our current vibration. If we are having difficulty deciding and our mind cannot make sense of where to go, Celestite is here to connect us to our spiritual guides. The extra support strengthens our intuition and we begin to realize that there is no such thing as the correct path – we could choose any one of them and be exactly where we needed to be.

Find your way to harmony whenever life's decisions have you questioning with Celestite by your side in:
• Reiki (see page 182)
• Divine light meditation (see page 157)

Connect to spirit with Golden Healer Quartz, page 145
Deepen intuition with Enhyrdo Quartz, page 160

Mesolite

"Love radiates out from my being, connecting me to my community."

Mesolite

QUALITY	Collaborative, Communicative, Moving
CHAKRA	Heart, Crown
FOCUS	Stepping out of your comfort zone, Working together to manifest collective visions, Spiritual love

Needing help or support is often seen as a weak trait. It makes us prone to offer help to others, but rarely ask for it ourselves. The stigma around receiving is so strong and shameful we go out of our way to avoid situations where we may be pushed outside our comfort zone.

Anytime shame prompts us to move away from an experience, we should channel Mesolite's energy. Formed in the voids of Basalt veins, Mesolite's delicate form cannot exist without support. It is no less powerful, magical, or mesmerizing because of Basalt's help. We can learn how to similarly collaborate and develop a partnership that manifests an even more brilliant collective vision.

If you're resistant to receiving help, let Mesolite reframe the stigmas around support into opportunities for collaboration. When we learn to communicate our ideas, hopes, dreams, and needs to our community, we increase the possibility that we're able to make them happen.

Embrace community support and shift the hold shame has over you with Mesolite in:
• Hand-holding meditation (see page 157)
• The gaze (see page 238)

Team player? Go to Jadeite, page 61
Shake the shame with Blue Lace Agate, page 168

Fairy Stone

Magic, Joyful, Free-spirited	**QUALITY**
All	**CHAKRA**
Rediscovering the mysticism of life, Breaking free from routine, Taking time for play	**FOCUS**

Our world is a multi-layered ecosystem of divine energy. We only see a fraction of its energetic expression. The more our lives are spent indoors, the greater the distance we feel from nature's loving energy. We begin to lose sight of the magic and mystery that make up our world, opting instead for the distractions and diversions that are readily available with just one click.

Fairy Stone invites us out to play, helping us break out of the routine that prevents us from appreciating the magic of nature. It rekindles our sense of wonder and joy, encouraging us to embrace a light-hearted and free energy.

Our souls long for adventure and play. It's the essence that makes us feel alive. Fairy Stone is the sweet surprise that nature tosses our way to shake things up. Taking time to reset and rediscover the world inspires our hearts and minds, helping to keep us focused when we get back to the daily grind.

Commune with the energy of Fairy Stone whenever you are feeling too serious. Incorporate it into:
- Forest bathing (see page 52)
- Heart flow (see page 31)

WATER

Fairy Stone

"The more time I take to let my spirit play, the more I feel renewed."

Feeling stiff? Loosen up with Chlorite Quartz, page 203
Tap into your inner child with Datolite, page 111

Exploring the inner landscape

Whenever you feel disconnected, lost, in need of guidance, or desire a vibrational boost, these stone practices reconnect you with the etheric and spiritual essence of your inner landscape. Feel your way through them sequentially for a powerful reset, or individually for a mindful tune-up.

Sense writing

Strengthening sensory awareness encourages presence. Being present provides clarity and connection. Cultivate a connection to the here and now through energetic journalling.

- Intuitively choose a stone and hold it in your hands while meditating for five minutes.
- With each breath, focus your awareness on the space around you, noticing what you sense.
- Open your eyes and begin writing using only sensory statements (I see, I feel, I hear, I taste, I smell) to describe your perceptions.
- Take it deeper by applying the sensory statements to your energetic vibration (my energy sees, my energy feels, my energy hears, my energy tastes, my energy smells). Just let your intuitive thoughts surface.
- How has awareness of your environment, both physical and energetic, shifted your sense of connection?

Crystal reading

Use this energetic assessment to see how your energy is flowing, to ask questions, set intentions, and find inspiration.

- Create a crystal grid using your intuition.
- Close your eyes and centre your energy by taking several deep breaths.
- Once you feel grounded, think about the question, situation, or intention that you would like more guidance navigating. Let whatever surfaces in your mind find space within your heart to be acknowledged.
- Open your eyes and identify the stones that jump out at you.
- Pay attention to the patterns, shapes, and connections you see between the stones. Go deeper into their individual qualities by exploring them in this book.
- Piece together your impressions to uncover a crystal message offering unique insight into your experience.

Crystal contemplation

The stones we are drawn to reveal multitudes about us. Even more so when we allow that wisdom to bubble up without first distracting our minds by what we think we already know about the stone. Tap into your own guidance by free writing with just the stone's visual to inspire you.

- Intuitively select a stone from this book or your personal collection.
- Focusing on its physical form, begin writing whatever comes to mind for five minutes.
- Note any key themes or revelations that emerged as you wrote.
- Now look up the stone's energetic properties, qualities, and uses.
- Compare and contrast the stone's associated elements with your experience.
- Reflect on your discoveries. What have you learned about yourself and your vibration in this moment? How can this guide you?

Aura meditation

A crystal aura meditation illuminates our energetic hues and empowers us to move forwards with conscious intention and awareness.

- Close your eyes and begin breathing in a slow, deep rhythm. Envision the colour of your aura as a glowing light around you.
- Keep the rhythm of your breath smooth as you visualize the qualities of your aura transforming into sparkling, vibrant crystal vibrations.
- As you connect to the crystalline essence of your aura, with eyes still closed, let it guide you to a crystal in this book.
- Allow this crystal to reveal what energies could support or are present for you in this moment.
- Channel this vibration as often as you need throughout the day to reconnect to and feel empowered by this crystalline wisdom.

Amethyst Flower

"I see myself as I am;
beautiful, magical,
radiant."

Kunzite

"My whole essence
is an expression of
unconditional love."

Amethyst Flower

Radiant, Reflective, Magical	**QUALITY**
Heart, Crown	**CHAKRA**
Seeing the beauty in oneself, Sharing one's divine gifts, Witnessing small signs from the universe	**FOCUS**

There's immense discomfort in acknowledging beauty. We see it as finite and fleeting. So anytime we regard others' beauty favourably, we assume it means ours is less so. Staring into a mirror, it is easy to fixate on the imperfections, overlooking that true beauty emerges from within as an expression of divine energy.

We forget that we are mirrors for each other and, as mirrors, we reveal the beautiful complexity of our expression. We see our gifts, strengths, and dreams alongside our weaknesses, frustrations, and fears. Amethyst Flower, with one side that sparkles and another that seems rather dull in comparison, shows us how the two are part of the same whole. Accepting ourselves fully allows our beauty to radiate out naturally.

Look in the mirror and regard yourself with love. Can you do this without judging what you see? Follow Amethyst Flower's lead and allow the divine energy within to radiate out. Let your inner beauty be a beacon of inspiration and love.

Use Amethyst Flower whenever you forget your magnificence in:
- The gaze (see page 238)
- Serene silence (see page 238)

Cultivate spiritual gifts with Enhydro Quartz, page 160
Uncover the universe's signs with Sapphire, page 176

Kunzite

Loving, Renewing, Unconditional	**QUALITY**
Heart	**CHAKRA**
Connecting to divine love, Learning to surrender, Cultivating inner peace	**FOCUS**

There's an energetic turbulence flowing through our communities that leaves so many feeling insufficient. We look in the mirror and wonder – "Am I enough, am I doing enough, what's preventing me from being seen?" All the effort expended in a search for connection and witnessing leaves us feeling weak.

In moments like these, where we feel weary and alone, Kunzite connects us to the infinite source of love that is all things. We rediscover our innocence and surrender ourselves to divine love. The roots of resistance fade away and obstacles transform into exciting opportunities for growth.

Whenever you need instant peace or a reminder that you are enough, let Kunzite's gentle yet powerful vibration wash over you like a waterfall. Your energy will begin to emanate endless, unconditional love. As it pours around you and nourishes each cell, you'll feel each chakra pull into alignment with your heart, leaving your spirit centred and renewed.

Transform your energy into divine love with Kunzite in:
- Heart flow (see page 31)
- Divine light meditation (see page 157)

Feeling love? Let it overflow with Sillimanite, page 170
Struggling with self-worth? See Gold, page 119

Iron Quartz

QUALITY	Cosmic, Patient, Reflective
CHAKRA	Root, Sacral, Crown
FOCUS	Appreciating the expansiveness of the universe, Remembering our divinity, Opening the heart

During the day, the sky feels close and knowable. The sun rises, the clouds roll by, weather happens. We seldom look up and think about what else is beyond the ether. It is only when the sun sets, giving space for the moon and the stars to be seen that we open up to the expansiveness of the universe.

Expanding our earthly mind, Iron Quartz acts as a bridge into the unknown celestial world, bringing us that much closer to the divine. As one tiny planet among many, this awareness helps us appreciate our relationship to the cosmos. Embodying both a grounded and uplifting energy, Iron Quartz sweeps away sorrow and stress, easing the heart open and connecting us to our inner radiance.

Go out into the night and stare at the stars. Connect to the cosmic compass that guides our consciousness. How does it feel to be among such celestial magnificence? Iron Quartz brings it all back down to earth, illuminating the cosmos within, reminding us that we too are divine celestial beings.

Tap into your inner star with Iron Quartz. Let it inspire a greater connection to the universe in:
• Stargazing (see page 52)
• Divine light meditation (see page 157)

Feeling disconnected? See Purple Fluorite, page 167
Channel the divine with Botswana Agate, page 61

Herkimer Diamond

QUALITY	Amplifying, Compassionate, Transforming
CHAKRA	All
FOCUS	Expanding energetic expression, Illuminating the shadow, Releasing judgment

When our emotional expression comes out too big, we are quickly criticized by those who are uncomfortable with our feelings. Realizing there isn't room, nor is it safe for us to be as we are and feel as we do, the experience encourages us to keep ourselves contained. It's not easy to give ourselves grace.

The more we repress ourselves, the greater the probability that our emotions will explode under pressure. Herkimer Diamond releases us from the judgment that holds us back from experiencing and transforming through our energetic expression. Like a lightning bolt to the soul, the shadowy parts hidden within are nurtured with unconditional love. One by one, Herkimer Diamond helps bring them to the surface for release. Each time it does, our energy is expanded and space is created for us to be and to feel.

Be gentle with yourself as you identify those moments where you were forced to shrink. Reclaim your emotional expression with Herkimer Diamond. Let its energy transform any parts of you that you have been told were too much, into the very beauty that will amplify your soul.

Feel your way through Herkimer Diamond energy during:
• Serene silence (see page 238)
• Sunrise or sunset meditation (see page 31)

Embrace your light with Golden Topaz, page 51
For emotional expression see Aquamarine, page 160

Herkimer Diamond (embedded)

Iron Quartz
"The cosmos is within
me, I am divine."

Herkimer Diamond
"Everything I am
and feel is a valid
expression of my soul."

Optical Calcite

"My intuition is strong
and flowing, guiding me
through life."

Labradorite

"There is more to me
than meets the eye."

Labradorite

There's a sacredness in each of our souls. It is what draws us to each other, yet the light that illuminates the fire within may not hit at an angle that makes it possible for another to see. With the abrupt and impatient way we interact and move about the world, we often overlook and dismiss those whose fire isn't visible to our eyes.

The layers of Labradorite carry a powerful message about the complexity of our spiritual experience. Its energy is at once bold and discreet, alluding to our own moments when we move between confidence and fear.

Do you feel seen for all that you are? Are you quick to dismiss others without giving them a chance to shine? Let Labradorite remind you of the beauty within each of us, that may only come to the surface if the light hits us just right. Under its vibration we learn to be gracious with each other, remembering that the fire is there even if we can't see it.

Learn to appreciate each other's depths with Labradorite in:
• Walking meditation (see page 30)
• Hand-holding meditation (see page 157)

Strengthen community with Black Kyanite, page 27
Open your heart and mind with Amber, page 115

Optical Calcite

Intuition is an energetic muscle we all have access to that informs our direction and choices. Its ability to guide us through life is unparalleled. Expressed as quiet inspiration, hearing it proves challenging, especially when we spend most of our time responding to more tangible stimuli.

Whenever we feel lost, or the connection to our inner knowing feels dim, Optical Calcite steps in and activates our intuitive receptors, giving us the energetic coordinates to guide the way. The clarity it offers helps us explore life with a sense of adventure. Our awareness shifts from being contained in a room with no exit to one with open windows and unlocked doors.

Close your eyes and call upon your intuition. Can you feel its whisper awakening within you? If there's too much static to make it out clearly, let Optical Calcite help you tune in and reconnect.

It clears the spiritual airwaves, ushering you back into your soul to welcome in a new sense of self-discovery and exciting beginnings.

Find your way with Optical Calcite. Let it jumpstart your intuition in:
• Aura meditation (see page 213)
• Sunrise or sunset meditation (see page 31)

Embrace a new beginning with Aegirine, page 242
Tap into purpose with Leopard Skin Jasper, page 149

Howlite

QUALITY	Open, Thoughtful, Calm
CHAKRA	Third Eye, Crown
FOCUS	Relieves stress, Fortifies the decision-making process, Reboots one's energy

We spend most of our waking moments stimulated and engaged in thought. All the endless thinking, planning, wondering, worrying, anticipating, creating lists to keep it all straight takes up significant mind space. When does it stop? When do we get a moment just to be?

In a world as busy as ours, we must actively set aside time for our own stillness. Moments where there is nothing to do and no responsibility. Howlite cultivates these moments, freeing the mind of thought and worry. As we fall deeper into its meditative energy, our cellular body resets. Recharged and ready, our decision-making and follow-through are fortified, allowing us to approach anything that comes our way with an open mind.

When anxiety comes knocking at your door, remember to follow Howlite's cue – take a breath, slow down, let your stress calm. With your anxiety drifting away, you are free to embrace the intuitive boldness that follows.

Enjoy the boost of strength and soothed spirit Howlite offers in:
• Crystal reading (see page 212)
• Mineral nap (see page 182)

Recharged? Pop over to Crocoite, page 153
Find more stillness with Sapphire, page 176

Gwindel Quartz

QUALITY	Pivoting, Mysterious, Sacred
CHAKRA	All
FOCUS	Seeing all sides, Understanding complex and confusing situations, Illuminating the possibilities

Following is easier than charting our own path. When something has been done before, it's easier to do it again and make improvements or adjust course. We've been given the answers and only have to repeat them back. This rote behaviour keeps us locked in the same paradigm with no way out, stripping us of our unique vibration. We need to find a way to rediscover our inner pioneer who isn't afraid of the unknown.

Each twist of its body represents an awareness of the endless potential that exists at any given time. Facilitating an openness that links different possibilities and connects through time and space, Gwindel Quartz encourages us to march to the beat of our own drum. There is no definite answer, no expectation or deciding force that we feel from its vibration. Instead we are given free rein to explore all the angles simultaneously.

If you're ready to step into a new way of existing, there's no better time to begin. Unravel the knot of your current reality. Feel the awareness of everything all at once while you pivot away. Gwindel Quartz reinforces your ability to understand the complexity, creating and shaping reality on your own terms and in your own way.

Change your whole world with Gwindel Quartz. Feel its vibration unwind you during:
• Serene silence (see page 238)
• Mineral nap (see page 182)

See image on page 222

For liberated sensation see Peach Moonstone, page 142
Make sense of the potential with Sandstone, page 32

Howlite

"I take simple moments
to recharge so I have
the energy to act
with intention."

Selenite

"Peace flows through
me, connecting me to
my divine purpose."

Stilbite

"My dreams reveal the
wisdom of the universe.
I awaken inspired."

Gwindel Quartz

"I'm free to shift and
change whenever
I feel inspired."

Selenite

Peaceful, Calming, Purifying	QUALITY
All	CHAKRA
Realizing your soul's purpose, Finding serenity, Feeling the support of the universe	FOCUS

Learning to connect to our spirituality takes practice. The structure we set from the beginning helps to ensure we can build upon our foundation with confidence. It takes thoughtfulness and intention to create a foundation that can support us.

Selenite connects us to the divine light and peace within, creating the energetic backbone we need to build the rest of our practice upon. It strengthens our ability to receive messages from source, relaying them to each cell. The mind, body, spirit alignment that emerges instils serenity so we may fully embrace our destiny.

If things feel stunted or you're discouraged by the amount of force you're exerting to make something happen, cultivate a moment of peace with Selenite. It will purify your aura, clearing out all the debris, so you may fully align with your purpose. Your divine gifts will be more easily accessed and you see all the opportunities for your soul's expansion.

Find your spiritual structure and connect to the divine under Selenite's soothing vibration in:
• Reiki (see page 182)
• Serene silence (see page 238)

Uncover your spiritual gifts with Wulfenite, page 108
Learn the art of stillness with Ajoite, page 83

Stilbite

Activating, Adventurous, Celestial	QUALITY
Third Eye, Crown	CHAKRA
Spiritual journeying, Dream stimulation, Clearing out of unwanted vibrations	FOCUS

Our dreams are coded messages from beyond, rich with information. They come alive when we are deep in sleep and wisp away with the first flutter of our eyelids. Our memories of what happened are hazy. We are rarely able to remember them, let alone interpret their meaning.

Stilbite gives us the power to access the wisdom of our dreams more easily. An impulsive, wild energy, it takes us on an adventure through time and space. Under its vibration, we can experience the fantastic worlds only accessible through our dreams and learn to understand the cryptic messages hidden within them.

Take a nap and let yourself dream. What mystical places did you visit? What unusual messages did you receive? Stilbite exposes us to life's mysteries and opens us up to new ways of thinking and existing. It clears away the unnecessary vibrations that weigh us down so we may explore the spiritual realms more freely.

Enjoy Stilbite's adventurous energy in:
• The gaze (see page 238)
• Stargazing (see page 52)
• Stones on the body (see page 30)

Ready for astral travel? See Serpentine, page 136
More dreamwork? Flip to Silver, page 228

Galena

THE CRYSTALS

Even though we know that no one is perfect, we hold a lot of shame in our shadow – hiding parts of ourselves that we are afraid for others to see. Little things like poor choices we made at one time or another feel so incredibly significant that we begin to hide them from ourselves too. Losing touch with our true essence makes it difficult to connect with others. How could they know and love us if we're unable to do that?

Embracing our shadow is tough work. It asks that we see all aspects of who we are with love. Galena gives us the courage to face ourselves, to see ourselves as we are. When we do, the healing begins. With its support we can retrieve and nurture our forgotten essence.

Embrace a sense of wonderment towards your full expression. What are the things about you that are just pure magic? Can you allow your shadow to be a part of you too? Galena is here to shower you with love and support to release the hold shameful memories may have on you. Let it open your heart and remind you of your magical essence. You deserve to be loved for who you are.

Connect to your shadow self with Galena in:
• Gardening with stones (see page 52)
• Mirror gazing (see page 79)

Galena

"Every aspect of me
deserves to be loved."

Explore the shadow with Austinite, page 97
Integrate your essence with Alexandrite, page 241

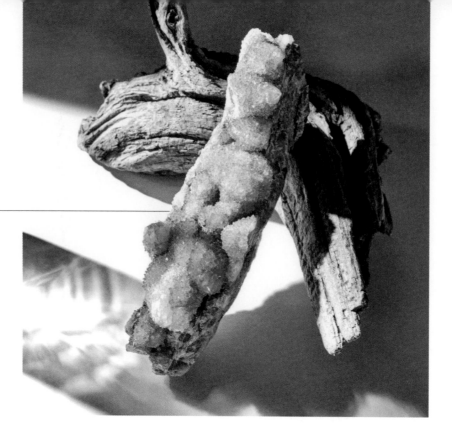

Spirit Quartz
"I nurture the divine gifts within, preparing them for the world."

Spirit Quartz

Transforming, Purifying, Amplifying	QUALITY
Solar Plexus, Third Eye, Crown	CHAKRA
Discovering your purpose, Developing your gifts, Amplifying your energetic expression	FOCUS

When the sky is grey, we often find ourselves feeling low and pensive. Have you ever noticed, though, that grey deepens the glow of the rainbow around it? The colours pop! We are able to see life with greater depth and that in turn lifts our energy.

There's nothing like a spiritually grey day to help us align more purely with our purpose. The vibration of Spirit Quartz purifies our aura to bring peace of mind and freedom from fear. It nourishes the gifts within, helping to hone and develop them until they are ready to be shared. Suddenly everything begins to click. We awake having a clear sense of who we are and what we are here to share.

This process doesn't happen the same way or on the same timeline for everyone. Spirit Quartz helps to harmonize our mind, body, and spirit, creating a supportive environment for each of us to transform as we are ready. When our gifts emerge, we must offer them up graciously.

Lean into Spirit Quartz to help your gifts emerge in:
• Mineral nap (see page 182)
• Creativity grid (see page 106)

Cultivate patience with Staurolite, page 66
Slow down with Mookaite Jasper, page 57

Grape Agate

"My actions lead to changes
that make the world a
better place for all to live."

Lemurian Seed Quartz

"All the answers
are within."

Grape Agate

Inspiring, Awakening, Considerate	QUALITY
Sacral, Solar Plexus, Heart, Third Eye	CHAKRA
Creating shifts in the paradigm, Seeing the intersections of life, Accepting responsibility for one's actions	FOCUS

The collective alarm clock has been ringing. We have kept on pressing snooze to the reality of life, where inequalities run rampant. In the haziness of opening our eyes, the bright sun streaming in the window feels intense, unsettling, challenging. Yet, we are running behind in our work to shift the direction of our world. It's time to wake up and get out of bed.

Courage, stability, and maturity are necessary to create deep shifts in collective consciousness. Grape Agate helps us find those qualities within, while also reminding us of the urgency. Its botryoidal shape, symbolizing the intersections of community, shows the importance of bringing people together to heal and grow through unity.

Recognize the way your actions affect the world around you. Are you willing to work together to address the issues plaguing humanity? Grape Agate encourages you to reflect on the different ways you can show up and make a difference in the world.

Channel the supportive and powerful energy of Grape Agate in:
• Community service
• Hand-holding meditation (see page 157)

For motivation flip to Mahogany Obsidian, page 141
Strengthen your community with Jet, page 147

Lemurian Seed Quartz

Knowing, Integrating, Expansive	QUALITY
All	CHAKRA
Releasing fear, Remembering our origins, Cultivating harmony	FOCUS

Restlessness arrives anytime we entertain fearful thoughts. Worry cloaks the energy of love in fear, making us feel disconnected from the divine. We forget where we came from and we struggle to remember knowledge that has been passed down to us. We've dug a hole around us that is difficult to get out of.

Lemurian Seed Quartz, with its awe-inducing striations, reminds us that everything we need is already within. It integrates all the emotional and spiritual consciousness passed on through our spiritual DNA with our physical and mental realities. Supported by its vibration we can climb out of the depths, filled with an illuminated perspective full of connection and expansion.

Are you trapped in a hole created by your own fear? Listen to the wisdom of Lemurian Seed Quartz to find your way out. Let it synthesize the information from your cells and unify your soul. When we remember that what we need is always there, fear fades away and love uplifts us.

Harness the illuminating energy of Lemurian Seed Quartz for the ultimate levelling up in:
• Mineral nap (see page 182)
• Serene silence (see page 238)

Open to your spiritual guides with Celestite, page 209
Let go of the need to know with Dolomite, page 71

Silver

QUALITY	Sensual, Whimsical, Ethereal
CHAKRA	Heart, Crown
FOCUS	Reconnecting to your passion, Embodied energetic devotion, Expressing love in its purest form

Over the course of a few weeks, the moon moves through each of its expressions from new to full and back again. Each moon phase is a revealing of something deeper, reflecting back with softness for us to witness. The consistency in its presence is a beautiful act of selfless devotion, an expression of love in its purest form.

On Earth the moon's essence is held in Silver, vibrationally embodying sensuality, whimsy, and ethereal introspection. Simply gazing at this mineral channels the moon's energy directly into our soul, offering access to sacred information to guide and inspire us.

What happens then when the moon is dark and we cannot make out its form? The moon's absence is a moment for us to rediscover ourselves, a moment to reflect and integrate. One glance at Silver reveals to us that we are our own celestial body radiating the bright light of the universe. It serves as a gentle reminder that we are expressions of the divine, and the loving energy we so desire is always there.

Let Silver reflect back to you your own inner light, mirroring the magic within, in:
• Love notes (see page 78)
• Moon phase grid (see page 106)

For your inner light see Spessartine Garnet, page 141

Embrace wisdom with Larimar, page 162

Morganite

QUALITY	Pure, Loving, Unconditional
CHAKRA	Heart, Crown
FOCUS	Understanding unconditional love, Nurturing one's relationships, Activating and cleansing the heart

When we begin healing, we often erroneously assume that there is an end point. We peel back the layers, hoping to arrive and be done. We may even think we've arrived, only to reach the heart centre. Once here, we realize that no matter how open our heart is, there is always more room for it to expand.

Understanding unconditional love means endlessly opening your heart to others. This may seem a daunting task, but Morganite's vibration activates our ability to go deeper into the heart, where we discover the essence of divine love. We remember our innocence, our truth, our purest expression of self. Let love in. Let it crack open the walls of your heart.

If you're having trouble surrendering, Morganite clears away any ego debris and re-instils its natural sweetness, enabling our hearts to unfold with ease. We will never be done unfolding, but who would want that when the alternative is to be completely immersed in divine love forever?

Open the heart to unconditional love with Morganite in:
• Ritual bath (see page 182)
• Hand-holding meditation (see page 157)
• Love notes (see page 78)

Soften the loving gaze with Ruby, page 50

Get bold with love. Jump to Blue Fluorite, page 172

Silver

"I am a mirror to the
divine, my essence
reflecting back
pure love."

Morganite

"My heart keeps
unfolding with
unconditional love."

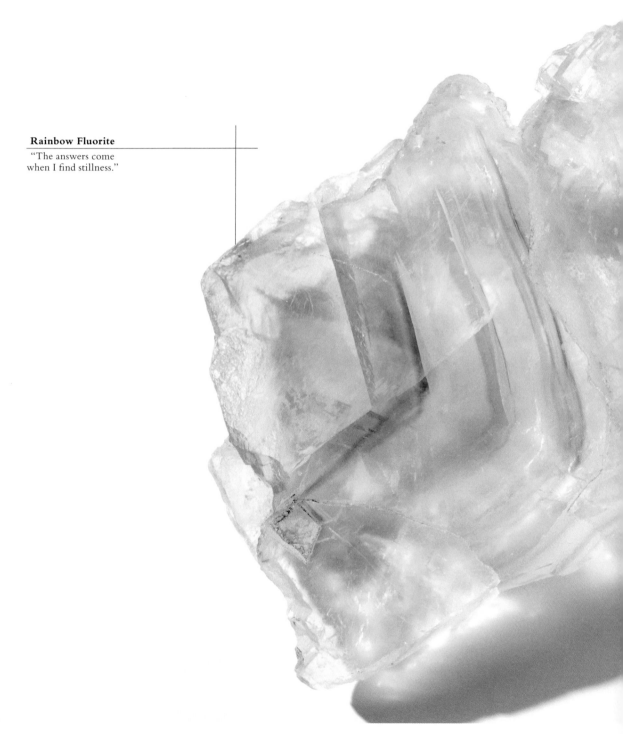

Rainbow Fluorite

"The answers come
when I find stillness."

Rainbow Fluorite

Protective, Uplifting, Nurturing	**QUALITY**
All	**CHAKRA**
Finding peace, Uncovering the hidden beauty, Cleansing the soul	**FOCUS**

Sometimes everything feels cloudy and it seems like there are no good options for the decisions we're facing. We struggle to see the beauty in the lessons, becoming more and more overwhelmed by our situation. Life can be challenging in the most confusing ways, leaving us with a frustration that doesn't seem to dissipate.

Wherever we find ourselves, Rainbow Fluorite parts the clouds in the energetic sky and offers its brilliance in nurturing rays that hug us tight. It reminds us to slow down so that the dust will settle and what we need will rise to the surface. Truth and clarity begin to shine into our lives, helping us make the best of our experiences.

When you are overwhelmed by life, hoping for a little clarity and direction, lean into Rainbow Fluorite. Let it cleanse and nurture your soul, giving you a moment's reprieve to gather your thoughts and listen to your heart. Keeping us safe and uplifted, Rainbow Fluorite guides us to feelings of peace, where we can witness the hidden beauty of our experiences.

Find your way with Rainbow Fluorite in:
- Ritual bath (see page 182)
- Mineral nap (see page 182)

ETHER

Find peace with Abalone, page 163

Embrace a new beginning with Anhydrite, page 180

Unakite Jasper

QUALITY	Insightful, Balancing, Grounding
CHAKRA	Root, Solar Plexus, Third Eye
FOCUS	Bridging the binary, Stimulating empathy, Expanding your mind

We move along the winding road navigating the many twists and turns that bring us in and out of view of our destination. The challenges ahead conceal our path and force us to rely on the support of our surroundings. Seeing ourselves as the other, outside of the community, makes this a difficult ask.

Life is a slow reveal, which allows us the time to connect with each other along the way. Whenever our focus begins to take shape as an "us vs them" mentality, Unakite Jasper, the spiritual architect, remodels the energy of time and space, creating a bridge of compassion that fosters sincere empathy.

Unakite Jasper expands our mind so we may see the way our experiences are woven together. Our pains stem from one root – our healing too comes from a unified source. This revelation moves us away from seeing ourselves as the saviours to others' problems towards seeing our problems as shared experiences that can only be addressed collectively. Together we can create peace and harmony. Unakite Jasper helps us construct the plan.

Call on Unakite Jasper to support you in:
• Breathwork (see page 156)
• Aura meditation (see page 213)

Unakite Jasper
"Your pain is my pain, mine is yours. Together we heal."

Break free from stereotypes with Austinite, page 97
Free emotional expression with Chrysocolla, page 175

Phantom Quartz

"I am a multidimensional
being, each experience
a step closer to my
spiritual ascension."

Phantom Quartz

Dynamic, Layered, Mystical	QUALITY
All	CHAKRA
Embracing change, Discovering the knowledge held within, Seeing the interconnectedness of life	FOCUS

There will be a moment in our own journey where growth takes a reflective pause, the length of which is unknown until it's over. This goes against our expectations. We assumed spiritual ascension to be consistent and linear. The process, however, is much more dynamic, ebbing and flowing in accordance with the unique lessons we are here to learn.

If we look at Phantom Quartz, we begin to understand that in these times of rest, etheric knowledge settles onto our energetic body, marking a period in our life we need to hold with special awareness.

We can never be certain how many times these moments will occur. Each one may invite an existential questioning that can only be overcome through complete surrender and trust. Phantom Quartz reveals the deeper purpose of those

shadows. We begin to see them as layers marking our personal growth and continual trust in the universe, welcoming the pauses with open arms.

Reveal the layers within and allow them to support your ascension with Phantom Quartz in:
• Stargazing (see page 52)
• Heart flow (see page 31)

Appreciate your unique path with Eudialyte, page 94
Go deeper into your essence with Ammolite, page 159

Azurite

"As we embrace the truth, we nurture the environment so we all may live in dignity."

Ametrine

"My mind is clear and present, I can accomplish great things."

Azurite

In our society, we are taught to fear another's success, as if it drained the well from where our own success is found. We are encouraged to hoard resources in the event that there won't be enough for us all. Seeing life through the lens of scarcity keeps us stuck in the status quo, unable to transcend.

What if our fears were revealed as unfounded? What if our hoarding was revealed as the direct cause of scarcity? Azurite lays down these truths and helps us see how beautiful the world would be if compassion were the foundation of our lives. Through its guidance we discover that our graciousness and generosity towards others radically shifts the way our society functions.

Close your eyes and reflect on where you feel fear in your life. Acknowledge all those fears with the truth and compassion that Azurite instils.

Wise, Truthful, Virtuous	QUALITY
Throat, Third Eye, Crown	CHAKRA
Developing compassion, Heightening spiritual awareness, Breaking free from social conditioning	FOCUS

Let it usher in energetic liberation where you can unchain yourself from scarcity behaviour.

Break free from societal conditioning with Azurite in:
• Breathwork (see page 156)
• Heart flow (see page 31)

For abundance mindset see Bumblebee Jasper, page 139
Explore the powers of truth with Blue Topaz, page 180

Ametrine

It's easy to get thrown off-course and fall out of balance with the lightning quick jolts of ideas that are exciting us all day long. Everything feels urgent, necessary, and possible. How do we know which of those impulses and mercurial movements of manifestation to follow? What do we do with them once we decide?

Corralling focus and soothing overactivity in the mind, Ametrine is our friend for balancing the flow of inspiration. It supports our decision-making process by keeping our energy aligned to what brings our hearts joy. We feel empowered as it purifies our aura, imparting the confidence to manifest our dreams with ease. Combining the essences of Amethyst and Citrine, it presents ideas in forms we can work with and build upon.

Allow Ametrine to clear away some of the extraneous ideas that are taking up space in your

Clearing, Activating, Focused	QUALITY
Solar Plexus, Third Eye, Crown	CHAKRA
Manifesting dreams into reality, Balancing the flow of inspiration, Making aligned decisions	FOCUS

mind. Follow your inspiration and keep the project on track with Ametrine's focused vibration. When we give ourselves room to work on what brings us joy, our dreams manifest more quickly.

Work with Ametrine in:
• Creativity grid (see page 106)
• Aura meditation (see page 213)

Forgot your why? See Chrysanthemum Stone, page 140
Need a boost of pure clarity? See Fire Opal, page 116

Heulandite

QUALITY	Calming, Meditative, Connecting
CHAKRA	Sacral, Heart, Crown
FOCUS	Releasing feelings of resentment, Opening up the heart, Finding your centre

Anytime we sacrifice what is important to us to please someone else, we make ourselves a martyr. We see our actions as noble and believe they make us superior to those for whom we've sacrificed. Habitually sacrificing to please others quickly becomes an addiction. The more we do this, the deeper the feelings of resentment take root, creating distance in our relationships.

Heulandite offers a different perspective – do everything from the love of your heart, not to please another. This outlook keeps us centred, helps us honour our boundaries, and ensures we are acting out of love.

Are you in a state of expecting others to sacrifice for you or have you been the one expected to sacrifice? Whichever side you tend to fall, restore balance with Heulandite. Its vibration will guide you back to centre and help open your heart for more honest connection. As you allow your desires to be heard, the resentment will fade and feelings of connection and support will take its place.

Release resentment and bring balance back into your relationships with Heulandite. Let it take you deeper in:
• Mirror gazing (see page 79)
• Love notes (see page 78)

Break free from habits with Sphalerite, page 150
Learn to collaborate with Chlorite Quartz, page 203

Angelite

QUALITY	Loving, Releasing, Nurturing
CHAKRA	Heart, Third Eye, Crown
FOCUS	Making the most of the moments we have, Navigating the twists of life, Connecting to those we've lost

We imagine life as endless time, that there will always be another day. Time is, however, relative to the life that lives it. Waiting around, assuming there will be another chance overlooks life's unpredictability. We are never promised a tomorrow, only a now.

How do we navigate the uncertain seas with grace? What happens if we miss our chance to say goodbye? Enter Angelite. Guardians, loving energy, and the delicate flutter of angel wings support us through all of life's turbulent experiences, especially the ones for which we need closure. It props us up, offering release and serenity so we can continue living life. Inspired by its loving support, we begin to reassess our priorities, shifting the way we show up in our relationships and making the most of every moment. Each of us is learning how to navigate the illusion of time. Our hearts ache with regret when we feel the effects of time poorly spent. In these frustrating moments, Angelite helps us reset.

If you are in the midst of loss, let the soft, sweet energy of Angelite envelop you in its angelic wings. There's no need to do anything at all, beyond remembering that no matter what, something greater is watching over you.

Appreciate the flow of life and reconnect with those you've lost with Angelite in:
• Gratitude practice (see page 78)
• Reiki (see page 182)

Grieving? Be soothed by Gold, page 119
Honour boundaries with Purple Fluorite, page 167

236

Heulandite

"My heart is open,
keeping me and my
actions centred in love."

Angelite

"My angels are all
around watching
over me."

Expansive mind

Between the moments of sound and action, we discover the transformative space of stillness. It is here where the mind resets by releasing the thoughts that keep it endlessly engaged, and we emerge emotionally soothed with deeper presence and clarity.

Golden channel meditation

Centre and harmonize your energetic flow to rekindle your connection to the divine. Holding a stone with an ethereal quality, envision your whole essence surrounded by a channel of golden light with each breath drawing the radiance simultaneously into each chakra, expanding them with the loving vibration of source energy. Your aura slowly begins to glow from the inside out meshing into the divine light of the universe, where you become the sun, the moon, the stars, and all the space in between. Relish this experience of cosmic divinity.

The gaze

Cultivate presence and energetic resolve by focusing your energy through the eyes. Have a crystal as a point of dedication – other options could be either a candle flame, an image, or a blank wall – in which you allow the visualization to emerge. Sitting with a straight, relaxed body, find your breath's organic rhythm, with your gaze focused ahead. Continue breathing and gazing until you feel ready to finish by closing your eyes and taking one last centring breath. Start with five minutes and slowly work your way up to twenty.

Serene silence

Embrace the silent serenity to give your mind the opportunity to breathe and become more receptive to source energy. Simply hold or channel your stone, close your eyes, pause your thoughts, and let your breath flow. Welcome any distractions that arise, enabling them to be absorbed by the rhythm of your breath. If the mind wanders, let your breath guide it back. Enjoy for as long as desired.

Clockwise from top: **Pyrite** page 126, **Snowflake Obsidian** page 27,
Girasol page 165, **Tangerine Quartz** page 129, **Datolite** page 111,
Morganite page 228, **Golden Topaz** page 51, **Amethyst** (centre) page 207

Alexandrite
"I am everything
and more."

Indigo Gabbro
"My intuition allows me
to experience the world
beyond the physical."

Alexandrite

There's a longing we have to be defined and digestible to those around us. We assume it will help us feel acceptance and create a box around our aura, keeping ourselves contained and predictable. Distilling ourselves down into a bite-size morsel is incredibly limiting and leaves no room for imagination or expansion.

Shifting colour based on the light that passes through it, Alexandrite shows us that things are not always what they seem. It reveals the ever-changing nature of the universe. We learn to harmonize our physical essence with the energetic, recognizing that we contain the infinite expression of the divine. There is no need to quantify or qualify with specifics when everything is relative to the moment in which we find ourselves.

Embrace your multi-dimensional complexity and your ability to shift. Alexandrite inspires the

Confident, Optimistic, Dynamic	**QUALITY**
Solar Plexus, Crown	**CHAKRA**
Harmonizes the physical and energetic bodies, Stimulates intuition, Purifies the soul	**FOCUS**

confidence and optimism to open up to the endless possibilities that exist for you, instilling a profound sense of spiritual prosperity.

Expand your form with Alexandrite whenever you feel contained. Let it inspire:
• Ritual bath (see page 182)
• Sunrise or sunset meditation (see page 31)

Gather the courage to be with Wulfenite, page 108
Move beyond either/or with Peridot, page 88

Indigo Gabbro

Our eyes are so focused on the external world, absorbing everything we see with passive curiosity. We are so attached to gathering information in this manner that we forget all the other possibilities and our minds are too stimulated to make sense of anything we see. Over time our capacity to discern depth is flattened into a one-dimensional view.

Going beyond sight seems strange. How do we look if not with our eyes? Indigo Gabbro guides us in letting go of all we thought we knew, encouraging us to embrace our intuition. Our sight is transformed into another kind of sense, one that perceives the hidden energy of all things.

Indigo Gabbro strengthens your intuition and teaches you how to pick up on the energetic vibrations of time and space. This gives you the ability to sense beyond the physical, stimulating

Magical, Expansive, Uplifting	**QUALITY**
Third Eye, Crown	**CHAKRA**
Enhancing intuitive abilities, Soothing an overactive mind, Facilitating spiritual awakening	**FOCUS**

the spirit and awakening you to the magic that is ever flowing in the ether.

Open your senses with Indigo Gabbro whenever you get stuck in the physical world. Particularly expansive in:
• Crystal reading (see page 212)
• Mineral nap (see page 182)

For multi-dimensionality see Desert Jasper, page 36
Reconnect with intuition with Lepidolite, page 77

Chrysoberyl

QUALITY	Forgiving, Generous, Diplomatic
CHAKRA	Heart, Third Eye
FOCUS	Promotes clear thinking, Helps you harness and direct your energy, Enables a full perspective

Forgiveness is the ultimate proof of abundance. To forgive means you are so full of love for yourself, for the world, for the ones who've caused you pain that you enter the neutral heart. Yet, truly offering forgiveness is a much more challenging act. Many of us think we've moved on and that we are unaffected, but we are still holding tight to the grudge.

The neutral heart is a tender space where we see all sides of the situation without ego. Chrysoberyl guides us along this challenging path, softening our rough edges and keeping our sight clear. We are able to go beyond the surface to the root of the experience and witness it with immense compassion. Expanding our awareness, Chrysoberyl creates space for all beings to simply be. There's no expectation. There's no critique. Just pure love.

What pains are you still holding? Look deep and honestly within, asking yourself if you're ready to surrender your hold on them and enter the neutral heart. Chrysoberyl will help you gain a full perspective so you can let go and move forward into a state of forgiveness, creating space for greater energetic abundance.

Allow Chrysoberyl to support you in finding peace from pains of the past. Useful in:
• Crystal reading (see page 212)
• Compassion grid (see page 106)

Let compassion flow with Shungite, page 196
No resentment with Watermelon Tourmaline, page 74

Aegirine

QUALITY	Clearing, Protective, Expansive
CHAKRA	Root, Crown
FOCUS	Fortifying the spirit, Eliminating unhealthy attachments, Cleansing the aura

We look to feel anchored in life, gently tethered so as not to drift away into the unknown. The constant weight creates a heaviness in our soul, pulling us down. It's a sensation of groundedness that we rely on to keep us secure, but can quickly turn to feeling restrained.

The challenge with anchors is to learn when to pull them up and move on. We become so comfortable with where we are that any hint at freshness overwhelms the senses. Aegirine brings with it a cleansing and protective vibration. It allows us to feel secure and open, ready to chart the unknown waters with renewed curiosity.

There's no shame in realizing you've become complacent in life. Switching up our routines and moving towards our dreams can cause anxiety. Holding tight to the familiar may give us momentary reprieve, but we know the cost – missed opportunities. Aegirine strengthens our spirit, giving us the fortitude to take a chance and discover the mystery that can only be found through exploration of the unknown.

Channel the vibration of Aegirine whenever your spirit needs the courage to pull anchor in:
• Aura meditation (see page 213)
• Ritual bath (see page 182)

For groundedness see Almandine Garnet, page 38
For serious soul purification try Sulphur, page 130

Chrysoberyl

"The more my heart
forgives, the more
space it creates for
abundance."

Aegirine

"The unknown may
seem daunting but I'm
ready for the adventure."

Barite

"My whole essence
is open to the hidden
vibrations of the
universe."

Barite

QUALITY	Dreamy, Intrepid, Aligned
CHAKRA	Heart, Throat, Third Eye, Crown
FOCUS	Releasing attachment to the physical world, Uncovering the secrets hidden in dreams

There's a whole world hidden beneath the veil of our eyes. The silent architecture of time and space that holds the wisdom of ages. Energetically we are drawn to it, but having focused our mind to the physical reality, find it difficult to access. Every now and then, an elusive whisper reminds us that there is something more out there.

How can we release the need for everything to be proven, release the need for our eyes to witness before believing? The awareness comes with support from Barite, a stone bestowing upon us a deep sense of independence from the physical world. Our senses attuned to things that cannot be seen, we develop the ability to discern their vibrations as if in a gallery of energetic sculptural reliefs.

Open your senses to perceive the greater energetic world around you. Are you able to feel the vibrations of the ether that exists between all things? Let this newfound receptiveness reveal the wisdom and empowerment that only comes from being able to see in depth.

Explore the ether with Barite. Try it in:
- Mirror gazing (see page 79)
- Crystal contemplation (see page 213)

Open up to the mystery with Botswana Agate, page 61
Rediscover your senses with Orange Selenite, page 33

Phenacite

Activating, Amplifying, Cleansing	QUALITY
Crown	CHAKRA
Expanding spiritual awareness, Purifying the aura, Connecting with the divine	FOCUS

We are ever-expanding beings. Each moment of our existence gently pulls our vibration to create a mystical essence that transcends our reality. When we close our eyes, we transport to a place where we become nebulous and morphing – pure energy. To exist in a perpetual state of flow is to be fully aligned and open. Some may call it enlightened.

Our energetic stream has ebbs that kink up and cause distraction, taking us out of alignment with source. Finding our way back is full of twists and turns. We may even feel disheartened by the process. Phenacite realigns our energy so we can focus on opening our spirit to the divine. Its support keeps everything flowing smoothly, releasing the pressure and reinvigorating our hearts. Activated by its vibration we can fully surrender into spiritual expansion.

Enlightenment doesn't need to be a solo endeavour. Welcome a little energetic activation from Phenacite to bring you back into a moment of awareness that allows you to transcend.

Open up with Phenacite's energy in:
• Divine light meditation (see page 157)
• Breathwork (see page 156)

ETHER

Phenacite

"I close my eyes and
see myself merge
with the universe."

For energetic collaboration see Mesolite, page 210
Feel your way through time with Dalmantine, page 91

Dravite

QUALITY	Grounding, Fortifying, Empowering
CHAKRA	Root, Sacral, Solar Plexus
FOCUS	Transmuting energy, Strengthening self-confidence, Building community connection

The world has increasingly become more fearful and isolated. Maybe we don't feel significant enough, maybe we don't see each other as significant enough. We are so uncomfortable with each other that we prefer to keep our interactions shallow, preventing any opportunity for real connection.

Sensitive to our shame and society's mores, we struggle to open up to each other. There is so much fear in being seen, in being connected. Transmuting these fears, Dravite soothes the soul and strengthens our self-image. We begin to emit a confidence that inspires vulnerable truth.

Hold the hand of someone you care about without saying anything. Let them feel the love in your heart flow down through your arm into your palm and into theirs. If you are feeling too raw and vulnerable, Dravite's supportive vibration instils in you the courage to connect. These moments of tenderness have the power to calm anxious feelings and remind us we are loved. There need to be more moments like them.

Cultivate deeper relationships with Dravite. Lean into its welcoming and accepting energy in:
• Hand-holding meditation (see page 157)
• Chakra balancing (see page 156)

Release your shame with Dioptase, page 105
Communicate with Chrysocolla, page 175

Tektite

QUALITY	Beyond, Otherworldly, Transformative
CHAKRA	All
FOCUS	Catalysing spiritual evolution, Expanding consciousness, Strengthening the soul

A lot of the spiritual evolution that occurs happens organically within us. We explore our selves and our connection to the divine. The movement is steadily progressive, looping back over what we have learned before cementing it into our consciousness. But for all this internal processing, we don't exist in a vacuum.

In much the same way that meteorites affect the Earth, we too are constantly reacting to stimuli outside of ourselves. These dramatic experiences shape us and catalyse our spiritual evolution in ways we never could anticipate. Tektite, a stone created when meteorites hit the Earth, with its otherworldly energy, acts as stimuli to move us out and beyond the inner self. We are thrust into situations, challenged beyond comparison, and given access to celestial wisdom that transforms us entirely. Once hit, we are never the same again.

It can be scary to know that these experiences are coming full force ready to make contact with your aura. It can be intense to feel the impact and be jolted into expanded consciousness. We may not feel ready, but Tektite strengthens our soul, teaching us how to welcome the blow. Replacing our fear with energetic gusto, we are ready for whatever new lesson this experience brings.

Welcome spiritual expansion with Tektite. It expands the soul in:
• Breathwork (see page 156)
• Stones on the body (see page 30)

Revisit your past lessons with Basalt, page 124
Release the need to prepare with Amber, page 115

Dravite

"I boldly open my heart and connect from a place of loving depth."

Tektite

"I am ever-learning, ever-evolving. Each experience expands my consciousness."

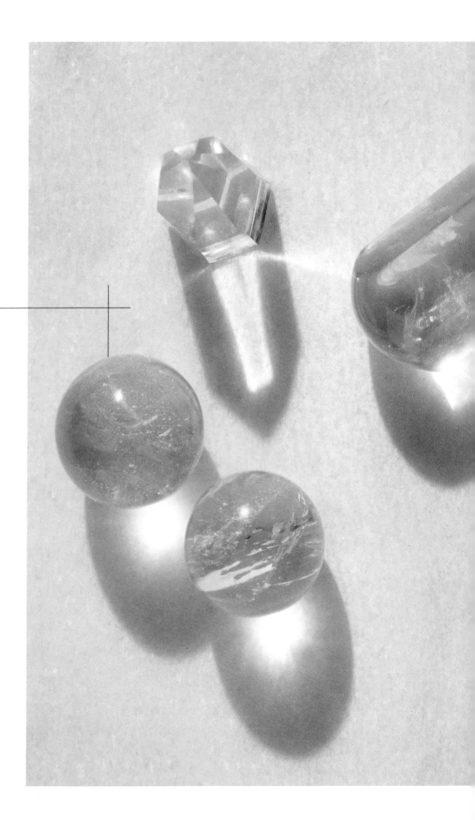

Clear Quartz
"I am I am I am."

248

Clear Quartz

Endless, Whole, Expansive	**QUALITY**
All	**CHAKRA**
Amplifying energy, Recognizing impermanence, Illuminating the possibilities	**FOCUS**

ETHER

The void is a space of endless possibility, pure expansiveness, and complete illumination. There's something alluring about its clarity and openness, something intense and overwhelming, too. We want to move towards it, but what will happen when we venture out into that space of impermanence? Our curiosity heightens the closer we get, when it suddenly becomes apparent that what we are looking at is ourselves.

Everything about us is displayed so purely, truthfully, raw, revealed - it can be painful to look at, to see everything we've been avoiding so brilliantly magnified. Acting as a beacon, Clear Quartz is both the light shining on us clarifying what we've been running from and the light guiding us home, back into ourselves. It magnifies those experiences that are looking for resolution, keeping them front and centre so we may learn, grow, and transform from them. Clear Quartz connects us to a deep stillness that amplifies our inner voice so we may know what is in alignment and move towards that with intention.

Seeing ourselves is deeply uncomfortable. We are both intrigued and unsettled. The more we avoid, the more painful this witnessing can be. Clear Quartz connects us with our deepest truth. Under its supportive vibration, we learn to appreciate the wisdom that arrives when we stop avoiding ourselves and embrace the beautiful impermanence of life.

See yourself fully with Clear Quartz in:
• Serene silence (see page 238)
• Mineral nap (see page 182)

Explore the beginning with Turquoise, page 46
Follow the possibilities with Sillimanite, page 170

Index